Contents

Thatch's Handbook of Political Ideology

By Charles Thatch

Absolute Monarchism

Absolute monarchism is a political ideology centered on the concentration of supreme power in the hands of a monarch who wields unrestricted authority over the state and its institutions. This form of government, prevalent in various historical periods and regions, differs significantly from other systems, such as constitutional monarchy or democracy.

Historical Context and Development
The roots of absolute monarchism can be traced back to ancient civilizations, where rulers claimed divine right and held absolute authority. However, it gained prominence during the Renaissance and Early Modern periods in Europe. Monarchs such as Louis XIV of France, Peter the Great of Russia, and Frederick II of Prussia exemplified absolute monarchism through their centralized control and assertion of royal power.

Key Characteristics
Absolute monarchism is characterized by several key features:

- Unrestricted Power: The monarch holds supreme authority, with no constitutional limitations or checks on their power. Their rule is considered absolute and unquestionable.

- Divine Right: Absolute monarchs often claim divine right, asserting that their authority is granted by a higher power. They are seen as the earthly representatives of God, justifying their legitimacy and authority.

- Centralized Control: Absolute monarchs exert centralized control over all aspects of governance, including legislation, administration, and judiciary. Decisions and policies are made by the monarch without significant input or oversight from other institutions.

- Patronage and Bureaucracy: Monarchs often employ a system of patronage, rewarding loyal subjects with positions of power and influence. A bureaucratic apparatus is established to implement the monarch's policies and maintain control over the state's functions.

Notable Theorists
Several theorists have contributed to the development and justification of absolute monarchism:

- Jean Bodin: Bodin, a French jurist and political philosopher of the 16th century, argued for absolute sovereignty in his work "Six Books of the Commonwealth." He emphasized the importance of a strong, centralized state led by an absolute monarch to ensure stability and order.

- Thomas Hobbes: Although not an explicit advocate of absolute monarchy, Hobbes' influential work, "Leviathan," presented a theory of absolute authority. Hobbes argued that a powerful sovereign was necessary to prevent the chaos and violence inherent in a state of nature.

- Jacques-Bénigne Bossuet: A French bishop and theologian, Bossuet wrote "Politics Derived from Holy Scripture," which provided theological justifications for the divine right of kings. He argued that monarchs ruled by divine mandate and that resistance to their authority was both sinful and disruptive to social order.

- Jean Domat: Contributed to the concept of "gallicanism," which maintained the primacy of the French monarchy over the Catholic Church within France. He advocated for a strong monarch who controlled both religious and secular matters.

Legacy and Criticisms
Absolute monarchism played a significant role in shaping political systems in Europe until the 18th century. However, it faced increasing challenges as Enlightenment ideas and the rise of nationalism questioned the legitimacy of unchecked royal authority.

The French Revolution in the late 18th century, with its call for popular sovereignty and the abolition of monarchy, marked a turning point in the decline of absolute monarchism. The concept of constitutionalism gained momentum, leading to the establishment of constitutional monarchies in several countries.

Enlightened Absolutism

Enlightened absolutism, also known as benevolent despotism or enlightened despotism, was a political ideology that emerged in the 18th century in Europe. It sought to combine the principles of absolutism, where monarchs held supreme power, with the ideas of the Enlightenment, which emphasized reason, progress, and the well-being of society. Enlightened absolutist rulers aimed to implement reforms and improvements for the benefit of their subjects while maintaining their absolute authority.

Enlightened absolutism was primarily associated with monarchs such as Frederick the Great of Prussia, Joseph II of Austria, and Catherine the Great of Russia. These rulers, influenced by Enlightenment thinkers such as Voltaire and Montesquieu, sought to modernize and improve their nations by implementing administrative, legal, educational, and economic reforms.

Key principles of enlightened absolutism included:

- Rational Governance: Enlightened rulers believed in the application of reason and scientific knowledge to governance. They sought to introduce efficient and rational administrative systems to ensure the effective functioning of the state.
- Social Reforms: Enlightened absolutists aimed to alleviate the social conditions of their subjects through reforms in areas such as education, justice, and welfare. They sought to promote education for the masses, create more equitable legal systems, and improve living conditions.
- Religious Toleration: Enlightened rulers often pursued religious toleration and sought to reduce the influence of the Church in secular affairs. They aimed to create more inclusive and tolerant societies, allowing religious freedom and promoting the ideas of religious pluralism.
- Economic Reforms: Enlightened absolutists recognized the importance of economic development and pursued policies to stimulate trade, industry, and agriculture. They aimed to improve economic conditions, alleviate poverty, and enhance the prosperity of their nations.

While enlightened absolutism brought about certain positive changes and improvements, it also faced limitations and criticisms. Critics argue that despite their intentions, enlightened rulers still maintained significant power and authority, often suppressing dissent and restricting individual liberties. Furthermore, the reforms introduced were often top-down and did not involve broader participation or representation of the population.

Enlightened absolutism represents a unique and complex blend of authoritarian rule and Enlightenment ideals. It reflects the attempt of rulers to reconcile their absolute authority with the progressive ideas of the Enlightenment. The legacy of enlightened absolutism remains an important chapter in the history of political thought and the pursuit of social progress.

Anarchism

Introduction

Anarchism is a political ideology that seeks to challenge and dismantle hierarchical systems of authority, including the state, capitalism, and other forms of oppression. Rooted in the belief that individuals should have the freedom to govern themselves and participate in decision-making processes, anarchism offers a vision of a society based on voluntary cooperation, mutual aid, and the abolition of oppressive structures. In this article, we will explore the core principles, historical roots, and diverse perspectives within anarchism.

Opposition to Authority and Hierarchies

At the heart of anarchism lies a fundamental opposition to authority and the concentration of power. Anarchists contend that hierarchical structures, such as the state, capitalism, and institutionalized forms of oppression, perpetuate inequality, restrict individual freedoms, and promote exploitation. Anarchists argue that individuals should be free to govern themselves and participate in decision-making processes that directly affect their lives, challenging the notion that authority is necessary for social order and progress.

Voluntary Cooperation and Mutual Aid

Anarchism promotes the idea of voluntary cooperation and mutual aid as alternatives to coercive systems. Anarchists advocate for decentralized, non-hierarchical forms of organization, where individuals and communities freely come together to meet their needs and address societal issues. Mutual aid involves individuals supporting each other, sharing resources, and working together for the collective benefit. This principle rejects the notion of competition and profit-driven motives, instead prioritizing solidarity and empathy.

Direct Action and Non-Hierarchical Resistance

Anarchism places a strong emphasis on direct action as a means to effect change. Direct action encompasses a range of tactics, including protests, strikes, civil disobedience, and grassroots organizing. Anarchists believe in taking action directly to challenge oppressive systems, rather than relying on representatives or intermediaries. Non-hierarchical resistance seeks to disrupt and challenge authority, highlighting the power dynamics inherent in hierarchical structures and demanding a more egalitarian and participatory society.

Social Justice and Liberation

Anarchism is deeply intertwined with the pursuit of social justice and liberation. Anarchists aim to dismantle systems of oppression based on factors such as race, gender, class, and other forms of discrimination. They recognize that hierarchies and power imbalances perpetuate systemic injustice, and advocate for the creation of inclusive, equitable communities. Anarchist feminism, queer anarchism, and anti-racist anarchism are among the many strands within anarchism that focus on intersectional struggles and the fight against multiple forms of oppression.

Diverse Perspectives and Strategies

Anarchism encompasses a wide range of perspectives, tactics, and strategies. From individualist anarchism to collectivist anarchism, anarcho-syndicalism to anarcho-communism, there is a diverse spectrum of thought within the anarchist tradition. These variations reflect different approaches to achieving an anarchist society, from gradual social transformation to revolutionary action. Despite these differences, anarchists share a common commitment to freedom, autonomy, and the rejection of coercive authority.

Critiques and Challenges
Anarchism faces several critiques and challenges. Critics argue that the absence of centralized authority may lead to chaos and a lack of social order. Additionally, questions arise regarding the practical implementation of anarchist principles on a large scale and the management of complex social issues. Critics also contend that certain social structures, such as education and healthcare, may require coordination and organization that anarchism may struggle to provide.

Individualist Anarchism

Individualist anarchism places a strong emphasis on individual freedom, autonomy, and voluntary association. Rooted in the broader anarchist tradition, individualist anarchism advocates for the abolition of all forms of coercion and hierarchical authority, including the state, while championing the sovereignty of the individual.

While individualist anarchism shares a common opposition to authority with other forms of anarchism, it distinguishes itself through its focus on individual autonomy and self-determination. Individualists prioritize the sovereignty of the individual over collective action or social revolution, emphasizing that true freedom can only be achieved through the emancipation of the individual from all forms of coercion.

Notable individualist anarchist thinkers include Max Stirner, Benjamin Tucker, and Lysander Spooner. Their writings and ideas have contributed to the development of individualist anarchism as a distinct strand within the broader anarchist tradition. Today, individualist anarchism continues to inspire those who advocate for a society based on voluntary associations, individual freedom, and the rejection of coercive authority.

Mutualism

Mutualism is a political ideology within the broader anarchist tradition that emphasizes voluntary cooperation, mutual exchange, and the establishment of a society based on economic and social equality. Developed by Pierre-Joseph Proudhon, mutualism seeks to create a system where individuals can freely associate and exchange goods and services on equal terms.

At the heart of mutualism is the principle of mutual exchange. Mutualists believe that individuals should be able to interact and engage in economic transactions on the basis of fair and equitable exchanges. They advocate for a system of free markets, where prices are determined through voluntary agreements between individuals, without the presence of monopolies or exploitative practices.

Mutualists view property as a social construct and reject both private and state ownership. They argue for a system of possessive individualism, where individuals have the right to the fruits of their own labor and to possess the means of production directly used by them. However, they advocate for an equitable distribution of wealth and oppose the concentration of wealth in the hands of a few.

Mutualism places a strong emphasis on decentralization and self-governance. Mutualist societies are envisioned as consisting of voluntary associations and cooperatives, where decision-making power is distributed among individuals and communities. These associations would function autonomously and cooperate with others based on mutual benefit and solidarity.

Mutualism also embraces the idea of "free credit," which promotes access to capital without interest or exploitation. Mutualist banks would provide interest-free loans, fostering economic opportunity and equality.

Anarcho-capitalism

Anarcho-capitalism blends the principles of anarchism with the economic theories of laissez-faire capitalism. It envisions a society without a centralized government where individual freedoms are maximized, and all interactions are voluntary and based on private property rights and free-market exchanges.

At its core, anarcho-capitalism advocates for the abolition of the state and its monopoly on force. Instead, it proposes a decentralized society where law, security, and defense are provided by competing private entities, known as private defense agencies or private security firms. These agencies would offer their services on the open market, allowing individuals to choose the protection they desire, creating competition to ensure efficiency and effectiveness.

Anarcho-capitalists believe that the free market, left entirely to its own devices, would naturally allocate resources, regulate business practices, and resolve disputes through voluntary contracts and agreements. They argue that the absence of government interference would lead to increased prosperity, innovation, and personal freedom, as individuals are allowed to pursue their interests without regulatory constraints.

Critics of anarcho-capitalism argue that the absence of a central governing authority could lead to chaos and power imbalances, as private defense agencies might become de facto mini-governments themselves. Furthermore, they contend that anarcho-capitalism may exacerbate social inequalities, as those with greater resources and bargaining power could wield disproportionate influence in a market-driven society.

Another point of contention is the potential for a lack of accountability in an anarcho-capitalist system. Without a central authority to enforce laws and regulations, there may be little recourse for individuals who face harm or injustice from more powerful actors.

In practical terms, anarcho-capitalism has not been implemented on a large scale, existing primarily as a theoretical construct. However, some proponents argue that smaller examples of voluntary and market-driven communities, such as intentional communities or startup cities, can provide insights into the viability of anarcho-capitalist principles.

Anarcho-Communism

Introduction
Anarcho-communism is a radical political ideology that combines the principles of anarchism and communism. Rooted in the belief that hierarchical structures and private property are the root causes of social inequality and oppression, anarcho-communists envision a society without a state, where wealth is shared collectively and all individuals have equal access to resources. In this article, we will explore the key tenets and goals of anarcho-communism, as well as its potential implications for society.

Stateless Society and Direct Action
At the core of anarcho-communism lies the vision of a stateless society, where power is decentralized and decision-making is carried out through direct democracy and consensus-building processes. Anarcho-communists reject the idea of a centralized state, arguing that it inherently leads to hierarchy, coercion, and the concentration of power. Instead, they advocate for grassroots organization, voluntary associations, and community self-governance. Direct action, such as protests, strikes, and other forms of non-hierarchical resistance, is seen as a means to challenge oppressive systems and advance societal change.

Collective Ownership and Abolition of Capitalism
Anarcho-communism promotes the abolition of capitalism and private ownership of the means of production. It advocates for the establishment of a system where resources, land, and industries are owned collectively and

managed by the community as a whole. The aim is to eliminate social class divisions and ensure that everyone's needs are met without the exploitation and alienation associated with capitalist production. By dismantling the profit motive and replacing it with cooperation and solidarity, anarcho-communists envision a society free from the inherent inequalities of capitalism.

Mutual Aid and Voluntary Cooperation

Central to anarcho-communist thought is the principle of mutual aid. Anarcho-communists believe that human beings possess an inherent tendency towards cooperation and solidarity, and that these traits can be nurtured in a society devoid of oppressive structures. Mutual aid involves individuals voluntarily coming together to support one another, sharing resources, skills, and knowledge for the collective benefit. Anarcho-communists argue that this ethos of voluntary cooperation and communal care can replace the competitive individualism fostered by capitalist systems.

Freedom and Autonomy

Anarcho-communism places a strong emphasis on individual freedom and autonomy. Its proponents argue that true freedom cannot be achieved under oppressive systems that limit access to resources, perpetuate social hierarchies, and stifle self-determination. By dismantling oppressive structures and establishing a society based on cooperation and equality, anarcho-communism seeks to create the conditions necessary for individuals to develop their full potential and lead fulfilling lives.

Challenges and Criticisms

While anarcho-communism presents an inspiring vision of a liberated society, it faces certain challenges and criticisms. Critics argue that the absence of a centralized authority may lead to chaos, inefficiency, and a lack of coordination. Additionally, the practical implementation of anarcho-communist principles on a large scale remains a subject of debate and speculation. Anarcho-communists counter these challenges by emphasizing the importance of community organizing, voluntary cooperation, and the ability of individuals to self-manage their affairs without hierarchical structures.

Conclusion

Anarcho-communism offers a radical and utopian vision of a society. By advocating for a stateless society, collective ownership, mutual aid, and individual autonomy, anarcho-communists seek to address the root causes of social inequality and create a world based on cooperation and solidarity.

Anarcho-primitivism

Anarcho-primitivism is an ideological framework that calls for the dismantling of civilization and a return to a primitive, hunter-gatherer way of life. It is a radical critique of modernity and industrial society, asserting that these systems are inherently oppressive, ecologically destructive, and detrimental to human well-being. Anarcho-primitivists argue that by embracing a simpler, pre-civilization existence, humanity can achieve a more harmonious and sustainable relationship with the natural world.

At the core of anarcho-primitivism is the belief that civilization and its associated technologies have led to the alienation of humans from nature and from one another. Anarcho-primitivists contend that the development of agriculture, the rise of hierarchical social structures, and the advent of industrialization have resulted in the exploitation of the environment, the erosion of community ties, and the creation of systems of power and control. They view these developments as a departure from a more egalitarian, cooperative, and sustainable way of life.

Anarcho-primitivists advocate for a society that embraces a range of practices and values associated with pre-civilized cultures. They argue that indigenous peoples and hunter-gatherer societies, who lived in close connection with nature, offer valuable insights into alternative ways of organizing society. Anarcho-primitivists promote a return to decentralized, autonomous communities that rely on small-scale, subsistence-based economies and non-hierarchical social structures.

Critics of anarcho-primitivism argue that its proposed vision of returning to a hunter-gatherer existence is idealistic and impractical. They contend that it overlooks the advancements and benefits brought about by civilization, such as improved standards of living, medical advancements, and technological innovations. Critics also highlight the challenges of transitioning from a highly industrialized and interconnected world to a primitive society, including issues related to food production, healthcare, and infrastructure.

Despite these criticisms, anarcho-primitivism has influenced and contributed to wider debates about the environmental and social consequences of industrialization and the pursuit of unlimited economic growth. It has drawn attention to the destructive impact of human activities on the planet and has called for a reevaluation of our relationship with nature.

Anarcho-syndicalism

Anarcho-syndicalism is a political ideology within the anarchist tradition that combines the principles of anarchism with the tactics and strategies of syndicalism. It emphasizes the importance of workers' self-management, direct action, and the overthrow of capitalism and the state.

At its core, anarcho-syndicalism seeks to create a society where workers have control over the means of production and decision-making power in the workplace. It advocates for the establishment of industrial unions or syndicates, which are grassroots, democratic organizations that unite workers across industries. These unions serve as a means of organizing and mobilizing the working class to achieve social and economic change.

Anarcho-syndicalists believe in the transformative potential of direct action, which involves workers engaging in strikes, boycotts, and other forms of resistance to challenge oppressive structures and demand better conditions. They reject traditional political methods such as voting or lobbying, viewing them as perpetuating existing power structures.

Another key aspect of anarcho-syndicalism is its opposition to capitalism and the state. Anarcho-syndicalists envision a society where economic production is based on cooperative and federated workplaces, organized through voluntary associations of workers. They argue that the state, as a coercive institution, perpetuates social inequality and maintains the interests of the ruling class. Anarcho-syndicalists advocate for the abolition of the state and the establishment of a decentralized, self-governing society.

Anarcho-syndicalism has played a significant role in labor movements around the world. Notable examples include the Spanish CNT during the Spanish Civil War and the Argentine FORA. Anarcho-syndicalist principles continue to influence labor activism today.

Authoritarian Capitalism

Authoritarian capitalism is an economic and political system that combines elements of a free-market economy with an authoritarian regime. In this model, the government maintains tight control over political power while allowing significant economic freedom for businesses and markets. The system often emphasizes law and order, stability, and centralized authority, which is seen as necessary to achieve economic growth and development.

One notable example of authoritarian capitalism was seen during Augusto Pinochet's rule in Chile (1973-1990). Following a military coup in 1973, Pinochet established a dictatorship, suppressing political opposition, and restricting civil liberties. However, his regime also implemented economic reforms inspired by the "Chicago Boys," a group of Chilean economists trained at the University of Chicago.

Pinochet's economic policies included privatizing state-owned industries, deregulating markets, and liberalizing trade. These measures aimed to attract foreign investment, increase competition, and promote economic growth. While these reforms resulted in economic growth and reduced inflation, they also led to significant income inequality and social disparities.

Critics of authoritarian capitalism argue that the concentration of economic wealth in the hands of a few, combined with a lack of political freedoms and democratic checks, can lead to abuses and exploitation. The model often prioritizes economic growth and stability over social welfare and human rights.

Authoritarian Conservatism

Authoritarian conservatism is a political ideology that combines elements of conservatism with an emphasis on strong and centralized authority. It advocates for traditional values, social order, and stability, often relying on a powerful government to enforce these principles. Unlike other conservative strains that prioritize limited government intervention, authoritarian conservatism supports a more assertive role for the state in preserving traditional institutions and moral values. Authoritarian conservatives may view more liberal forms of conservatism as inadequate to preserve traditional values and social order in the face of coordinated activism and social change.

One of the defining characteristics of authoritarian conservatism is its commitment to maintaining social hierarchies and traditional norms. It often opposes social changes, such as gay rights, gender equality, and progressive cultural shifts, viewing them as threats to the established order and moral fabric of society. Authoritarian conservatives often advocate for restrictive social policies and censorship to uphold what they see as a cohesive and stable societal structure.

Religion plays a significant role in many authoritarian conservative movements. The fusion of religious beliefs with political ideology reinforces the commitment to preserving traditional values and cultural practices. This alignment can be seen in countries where religious conservatism influences policy decisions on issues such as abortion, marriage, and education.

In terms of governance, authoritarian conservatism emphasizes the need for strong leadership and often supports a charismatic or dominant leader figure who can effectively enforce traditional values and maintain order.

Authoritarian conservatism can also exhibit nationalist tendencies, placing a strong emphasis on preserving national identity, culture, and sovereignty. This often manifests in policies promoting border control, protectionist trade measures, and opposition to international agreements that may be seen as undermining national interests.

As a political ideology, authoritarian conservatism exists in various forms and degrees across different countries and contexts. It has shaped the policies and platforms of numerous political parties and leaders worldwide, influencing governance and societal values in both positive and concerning ways.

Ba'athism

Ba'athism is a political ideology that originated in the early 20th century in the Arab world, primarily in Syria and Iraq. It was founded by Michel Aflaq, a Syrian philosopher, and Salah al-Din al-Bitar, a Syrian politician, with the aim of promoting Arab nationalism, secularism, and socialism.

The ideology of Ba'athism centers on the notion of Arab unity, seeking to create a unified Arab state or a pan-Arab nation that transcends existing borders and divisions in the Arab world. Ba'athists advocate for the rejection of colonialism, foreign intervention, and imperialism while promoting Arab self-determination and sovereignty.

One of the core principles of Ba'athism is secularism, emphasizing the separation of religion and the state. It envisions a society where religious identity does not dictate political governance, and instead, citizenship and equal rights are prioritized over sectarian or religious affiliations.

Another key aspect of Ba'athism is its commitment to socialism and social justice. It seeks to address socio-economic disparities, promote public ownership of key industries and resources, and implement policies that prioritize the welfare of the broader population.

Ba'athism also emphasizes the importance of leadership and organization. The ideology advocates for a vanguard party, the Arab Ba'ath Socialist Party, which is tasked with guiding the nation toward its goals of unity, secularism, and socialism. This centralization of power has led to criticism of Ba'athist regimes for their authoritarian tendencies and suppression of dissent.

Historically, Ba'athism has been associated with political movements and governments in Syria, Iraq, and other Arab countries. However, the implementation of Ba'athist policies has been met with mixed success, with some regimes accused of human rights abuses and failed economic policies.

Caesarism

Caesarism takes its name from Julius Caesar, the renowned Roman general and statesman. It refers to a system of rule characterized by the concentration of power in the hands of a charismatic leader who exercises strong authority and often displays authoritarian tendencies. While not a fully developed political theory, caesarism is often associated with the cult of personality and the dominance of a single leader.

Caesarist leaders typically exhibit certain characteristics:

- Strong Leadership: Caesarist leaders possess charismatic qualities and demonstrate a strong and decisive leadership style. They project an image of strength, authority, and determination, which appeals to the masses.
- Centralization of Power: Caesarism involves the consolidation of power in the hands of the leader. They may weaken or bypass established institutions and concentrate decision-making authority in their own office.
- Populist Appeal: Caesarist leaders often appeal to the sentiments and aspirations of the masses. They position themselves as champions of the people, promising to address their grievances and fulfill their desires for change and progress.
- Suspension of Norms: Caesarist leaders may disregard or manipulate established norms, rules, or even constitutional limits to maintain their grip on power. They often prioritize their own interests and agenda above all else.

Caesarism has historical roots in ancient Rome, where Julius Caesar's rise to power and subsequent transformation of the Republic into a dictatorship exemplified these characteristics. Throughout history, several leaders and movements have been labeled as caesarist, including Napoleon Bonaparte and certain 20th-century dictators.

Caesarism is often viewed as a double-edged sword. On one hand, it can bring stability and efficiency, especially during times of crisis, by providing a strong leader capable of making swift decisions. On the other hand, it carries the risk of autocracy and the potential for abuse of power.

Capitalism

Capitalism, as an economic and political system, has exerted a profound influence on societies around the world. With its emphasis on private ownership, market competition, and profit maximization, capitalism has shaped the course of history and underpinned the development of modern economies. In this article, we will explore the political influence and ideological aspects of capitalism.

One of the key political influences of capitalism lies in its promotion of individual liberty and economic freedom. Capitalism asserts that individuals should have the right to own and control private property, engage in voluntary exchange, and pursue their own economic interests. This ideology has often been associated with liberal democracy, as it aligns with principles such as limited government interference, free markets, and individual rights. Capitalism's emphasis on private enterprise and entrepreneurship has fueled innovation, economic growth, and technological advancements, leading to increased standards of living for many people.

Capitalism also has significant ideological dimensions that have shaped societies and political discourse. Some of the main ideological aspects of capitalism include:

- Free Market Economics: Capitalism promotes the idea of a free market, where the forces of supply and demand determine prices and allocate resources. The belief is that in a competitive market, individuals and businesses acting in their self-interest will lead to optimal outcomes and the most efficient allocation of resources.

- Economic Individualism: Capitalism values individualism and the pursuit of self-interest. It holds that individuals are best suited to make decisions regarding their own economic choices, and that these choices collectively drive economic growth and prosperity.

- Private Property Rights: Capitalism places a strong emphasis on the protection of private property rights. The idea is that individuals should have the right to own, use, and transfer property, providing them with incentives to invest, innovate, and accumulate wealth.

- Meritocracy: Capitalism often promotes the concept of meritocracy, where success and social status are seen as rewards for individual talent, hard work, and ability. The belief is that in a capitalist society, individuals have the opportunity to rise or fall based on their own merits.

- Economic Growth and Prosperity: Capitalism's focus on economic efficiency and profit maximization is driven by the belief that a vibrant and expanding economy benefits society as a whole. Capitalist systems seek to generate wealth and improve living standards through economic growth and the accumulation of capital.
- Minimal State Intervention: Capitalism often advocates for limited government intervention in the economy. It argues that the role of the state should be primarily to protect property rights, enforce contracts, maintain a stable legal framework, and provide necessary infrastructure and public goods.

While capitalism has brought many benefits, it also faces criticism and scrutiny. Critics argue that capitalism can lead to income inequality, exploitation of labor, environmental degradation, and the concentration of wealth and power in the hands of a few. In response, various forms of regulation, social safety nets, and welfare policies have been implemented in many capitalist economies to address these concerns and mitigate the negative impacts of capitalism.

Christian Democracy

Christian democracy is a political ideology that seeks to integrate Christian values and principles into democratic governance. It emerged in Europe in the late 19th and early 20th centuries as a response to the challenges posed by industrialization, secularism, and the rise of socialist and communist movements.

Christian democratic parties and movements prioritize the application of Christian social teachings and ethics to politics and public policy. They emphasize values such as human dignity, solidarity, subsidiarity, and the common good. Christian democracy seeks to bridge the gap between religious beliefs and democratic principles, aiming to create a just and harmonious society.

One of the key tenets of Christian democracy is the belief in the inherent dignity and worth of every individual. This principle is rooted in Christian teachings on the sanctity of life and the belief that all people are made in the image of God. Christian democrats advocate for the protection of human rights, social justice, and the promotion of policies that alleviate poverty, inequality, and discrimination.

Another central aspect of Christian democracy is the emphasis on solidarity and community. Christian democrats believe in the importance of fostering strong social bonds and promoting a sense of shared responsibility. They advocate for policies that support families, strengthen communities, and encourage cooperation among different groups and sectors of society.

Subsidiarity is a key principle of Christian democracy, emphasizing that decision-making should occur at the most local and appropriate level possible. This principle recognizes the importance of local communities and institutions in addressing societal challenges. Christian democrats advocate for decentralized governance structures that empower local communities and promote active citizen participation.

Christian democracy also emphasizes the concept of the common good. It holds that policies and decisions should prioritize the well-being and flourishing of society as a whole, rather than just individual interests. Christian democratic parties often promote policies that aim to balance individual rights with the broader social needs and responsibilities.

Christian democracy has had a significant impact on the political landscape in several countries, particularly in Europe. Christian democratic parties have been instrumental in shaping welfare policies, labor rights, and social programs. They have also played a crucial role in fostering social dialogue and reconciliation, especially in countries recovering from political upheaval or conflict.

It is important to note that Christian democracy is not a homogeneous ideology, and there can be variations in its interpretation and application across different regions and countries. While it is rooted in Christian values, the specific policies and positions of Christian democratic parties can vary depending on local contexts, cultural influences, and the prevailing political environment.

In conclusion, Christian democracy is a political ideology that seeks to integrate Christian values and principles into democratic governance. It emphasizes human dignity, solidarity, subsidiarity, and the common good. Christian democratic parties aim to bridge the gap between religious beliefs and democratic principles, advocating for social justice, community building, and the pursuit of the common good. While it has had a significant impact on the political landscape, the interpretation and application of Christian democracy can vary across different regions and countries.

Christian Nationalism

Christian nationalism is a political and cultural ideology that seeks to fuse Christian religious beliefs with the identity and governance of a nation. It posits that a country's success and moral standing are intrinsically tied to adherence to specific interpretations of Christian principles. Supporters of Christian nationalism often argue for the establishment of policies aligned with their religious beliefs and seek to promote Christianity's influence in various aspects of public life.

Proponents of Christian nationalism believe that incorporating Christian values into the nation's laws and institutions will lead to a more righteous and cohesive society. They advocate for prayer in schools, the display of religious symbols in public spaces, and policies aligned with conservative Christian beliefs on issues such as abortion and homosexuality.

Christian nationalism is not a monolithic ideology, and its manifestations can vary widely across different countries and contexts. In some cases, it can intersect with populist and nativist movements, where the defense of Christian identity is intertwined with a broader nationalist agenda.

Christian Socialism

Christian socialism is an ideological framework that seeks to reconcile the principles of Christianity with socialist economic and political ideas. It asserts that the teachings of Jesus Christ and the values of the Christian faith are compatible with the pursuit of social and economic justice, collective ownership, and the establishment of a more egalitarian society. Christian socialists argue that the principles of love, compassion, and solidarity found in Christianity require active engagement in addressing social and economic inequalities.

At the heart of Christian socialism is the belief that the Bible calls for the fair distribution of wealth, the eradication of poverty, and the promotion of social welfare. Christian socialists draw inspiration from biblical passages that emphasize the importance of caring for the poor, promoting justice, and challenging oppressive systems. They view Jesus Christ as a champion of the marginalized and an advocate for social transformation.

Christian socialists often support policies and initiatives aimed at reducing income inequality, providing access to healthcare and education, and ensuring fair wages and working conditions. They argue that such measures are not only morally right but also align with the broader Christian values of love, compassion, and stewardship.

However, proponents of Christian socialism argue that their ideology is rooted in a holistic interpretation of the Bible and a commitment to promoting human dignity and social justice. They emphasize that Christian socialism does not advocate for a purely materialistic agenda but rather seeks to address the structural and systemic issues that perpetuate poverty, inequality, and injustice.

Christian socialism has a rich history and has influenced prominent thinkers and activists throughout the years. It played a significant role in the social gospel movement of the late 19th and early 20th centuries, which sought to apply Christian ethics to social problems. Figures such as Walter Rauschenbusch and Reinhold Niebuhr were influential in articulating a Christian perspective on social justice and promoting a more equitable society.

Communism

Communism emerged in the 19th century as a response to industrial capitalism. While there are variations and interpretations of communism, they all share a common goal: the establishment of a classless society where the means of production are collectively owned and controlled by the community as a whole. In this article, we will explore some of the main political ideologies associated with communism.

See also: *Marxism, Marxism Leninism, Socialism.*

- Marxist-Leninism: Developed by Karl Marx and expanded upon by Vladimir Lenin, Marxist-Leninism is perhaps the most well-known variant of communism. It advocates for a revolutionary overthrow of the capitalist system by the working class. According to Marxist-Leninist ideology, a transitional stage known as the "dictatorship of the proletariat" is necessary to establish a socialist state. In this stage, a vanguard party represents the interests of the working class and guides the revolution. Marxist-Leninists emphasize central planning, state ownership of the means of production, and the eventual withering away of the state to achieve a classless, communist society.

- Maoism: Developed by Mao Zedong in the context of the Chinese Revolution, Maoism is an adaptation of Marxist-Leninist theory. It emphasizes the role of peasants in revolution and places a greater emphasis on rural-based guerrilla warfare. Maoists advocate for a continuous revolution to prevent the emergence of a new ruling class and stress the importance of mass mobilization and participation. Maoism also emphasizes self-reliance and a rejection of capitalist and imperialist influences.

- Trotskyism: Named after Leon Trotsky, a prominent figure in the Russian Revolution, Trotskyism offers a critique of the Soviet Union under Stalin and advocates for a more democratic and internationalist form of socialism. Trotskyists emphasize the importance of permanent revolution and believe that socialism should be spread internationally rather than confined to a single country. They oppose the concept of socialism in one country and advocate for workers' democracy and greater political rights within socialist societies.

- Anarcho-Communism: Anarcho-communism is a branch of anarchism that advocates for the abolition of all forms of authority, including the state and capitalism. It envisions a society where all goods and services are held in common and distributed according to the principle of "from each according to their ability, to each according to their needs." Anarcho-communists reject the idea of a transitional stage or vanguard party and believe that communism can be achieved directly through decentralized, voluntary associations and mutual aid.
- Democratic Socialism: While not strictly a communist ideology, democratic socialism shares some goals with communism. Democratic socialists advocate for the establishment of a mixed economy with both public and private ownership, along with an expanded welfare state to ensure economic equality and social justice. They aim to achieve socialism through democratic means and reject the notion of a violent revolution. Democratic socialists prioritize political and civil liberties and seek to build more equitable societies through electoral politics and grassroots activism.

Communitarianism

Communitarianism is a political ideology that emphasizes the importance of community and shared values in shaping society. It challenges the prevailing individualistic outlook of modern liberal societies and seeks to strike a balance between individual rights and the welfare of the community as a whole. One of the leading proponents of communitarianism is the Scottish philosopher Alasdair MacIntyre.

At its core, communitarianism contends that humans are social beings deeply embedded in a network of relationships and interconnected with others. It argues that individual identity and flourishing are intrinsically tied to the well-being of the communities they belong to, such as families, neighborhoods, and cultural groups. In contrast to the liberal emphasis on autonomous individuals, communitarianism stresses the importance of the "common good" and the need to prioritize the welfare of the community over pure individual interests.

Alasdair MacIntyre's influential work, especially in his book "After Virtue," delves into the significance of moral traditions within communities. He argues that ethical concepts are rooted in particular communal contexts and that a shared understanding of virtues is essential for ethical decision-making. MacIntyre advocates for a return to virtue ethics, which focuses on developing good character and moral virtues in the context of one's community, as opposed to adhering to abstract ethical principles.

Moreover, communitarianism criticizes the excessive focus on procedural justice and abstract individual rights, arguing that such an approach fails to address the complexities and context-specific nature of moral issues. Instead, it promotes deliberative democracy, where individuals engage in open dialogue and collaborative decision-making within their communities, aiming to find common ground and shared values.

Conservatism

Introduction
Conservatism is a political ideology that places emphasis on preserving traditional values, institutions, and social norms. Rooted in the idea of societal stability and continuity, conservatism seeks to maintain established customs, institutions, and hierarchies. In this article, we will delve into the core principles of conservatism and explore its historical development and key tenets.

Preserving Tradition and Stability
At the heart of conservatism lies a commitment to preserving tradition and stability. Conservatives value the accumulated wisdom and experience of past generations, emphasizing the importance of continuity and gradual change rather than rapid societal transformation. They believe that established institutions, such as family, religion, and the rule of law, play a crucial role in fostering social cohesion and order.

Social Order and Moral Values
Conservatism places great importance on maintaining social order and promoting moral values. Traditional social hierarchies, cultural norms, and religious institutions are seen as vital components of a well-functioning society. Conservatives argue that adherence to shared moral values provides a sense of stability, guides individual behavior, and preserves social cohesion.

Skepticism of Radical Change
Conservatives tend to be skeptical of rapid and radical change, emphasizing the potential risks it poses to societal stability and order. They argue that caution should be exercised when introducing sweeping reforms, as they can disrupt established institutions and traditions without necessarily improving the overall

well-being of society. Conservatives advocate for a prudent and gradual approach to change, grounded in respect for the lessons of history.

Nationalism and Patriotism

Conservatism often aligns with a sense of national identity and pride. Conservatives believe in the importance of a strong nation-state, asserting that a cohesive society and shared values are essential for social harmony and collective progress. National security and the protection of borders are considered fundamental to safeguarding a nation's interests and preserving its cultural heritage.

Criticism of Utopianism

Conservatives frequently criticize utopian visions that propose radical societal transformations based on abstract ideals. They argue that such grand schemes often disregard the complexities of human nature, undermine individual freedoms, and have unintended consequences. Conservatives advocate for pragmatic and realistic approaches that balance the pursuit of progress with the preservation of stability and established social structures.

The Influence of Conservative Thinkers

Throughout history, various thinkers have shaped the ideology of conservatism. Notable figures such as Edmund Burke, Russell Kirk, and Michael Oakeshott have contributed to the development of conservative thought. Burke, in particular, emphasized the importance of preserving tradition, gradual reform, and the value of inherited wisdom.

Burke vs De Maistre

The historical development of conservatism encompasses a broad spectrum of ideas and approaches. A notable comparison can be made between the more liberal conservatism of Edmund Burke and the throne-and-altar style conservatism of Joseph de Maistre. These two figures represent different strands within the conservative tradition, offering contrasting perspectives on the role of tradition, authority, and social order. While both wrote in opposition to the French Revolution, they did so with different concerns and approaches in mind.

Edmund Burke, often regarded as the father of modern conservatism, emphasized a more liberal and pragmatic approach. Burke believed in the value of tradition as a source of wisdom, but he also recognized the need for gradual reform to address societal challenges. His seminal work, "Reflections on the Revolution in France," criticized the radicalism of the French Revolution while advocating for a conservative response rooted in the preservation of existing institutions. Burke saw society as an organic entity, shaped by the accumulated wisdom of past generations, and believed that change should be incremental to avoid unintended consequences.

In contrast, Joseph de Maistre represented a more traditionalist and authoritarian strand of conservatism. He espoused the throne-and-altar ideology, which sought to maintain the close alliance between political and religious authority. De Maistre believed in the necessity of strong monarchical rule and the influence of the Catholic Church in preserving social order and moral values. He viewed tradition and hierarchy as indispensable for maintaining stability, arguing that human nature required guidance and restraint from an authoritative power. Unlike Burke, de Maistre was skeptical of liberal ideals such as individual rights and popular sovereignty, which he saw as potentially leading to anarchy and moral decay.

Despite their differences, both Burke and de Maistre contributed significantly to the development of conservative thought. Their ideas on tradition, authority, and social order continue to shape conservative thinking today. The liberal conservatism of Burke has influenced modern conservative thought by emphasizing the importance of limited government, individual liberty, and cautious reform. On the other hand, the conservatism of de Maistre has left its mark on conservative thinkers who emphasize the value of hierarchy, tradition, and a strong central authority.

In conclusion, the historical development of conservatism has encompassed a range of perspectives. The comparison between the more liberal conservatism of Edmund Burke and the throne-and-altar style conservatism of Joseph de Maistre highlights the diversity within the conservative tradition. These figures offer distinct views on the role of tradition, authority, and social order.

Classical

Classical conservatism, also known as traditional conservatism, is rooted in the preservation of traditional institutions, values, and social order. It emphasizes the importance of stability, continuity, and gradual change to maintain societal cohesion.

Classical conservatives believe in the wisdom of past generations and the value of established institutions, such as the monarchy, religious institutions, and the family unit. They view these institutions as foundational to the well-being and stability of society, providing a sense of continuity, hierarchy, and moral guidance.

Classical conservatives are skeptical of rapid social or political change, advocating for caution and respect for existing social structures. They prioritize the protection of individual liberties within the framework of established norms and traditions.

One key aspect of classical conservatism is the recognition of the limitations of human nature. Classical conservatives argue that humans are imperfect and driven by self-interest, and therefore, a strong government is necessary to maintain order and prevent the excesses of human behavior.

Fiscal

Fiscal conservatism prioritizes responsible fiscal policies, limited government spending, and lower taxation. It advocates for a balanced budget, reduced government debt, and a focus on market-driven solutions to promote economic growth.

Fiscal conservatives believe that a smaller government with limited intervention in the economy allows for more individual freedom and economic prosperity. They argue that excessive government spending and high taxation can hinder economic growth, discourage private investment, and lead to unsustainable levels of debt.

Fiscal conservatives often advocate for fiscal discipline, aiming to control government expenditure and ensure that public funds are allocated efficiently. They emphasize the importance of prioritizing essential services and avoiding unnecessary government programs and waste.

Libertarian

Libertarian conservatism combines elements of libertarianism and conservatism. It seeks to promote individual liberty, limited government intervention, and free-market capitalism while upholding traditional conservative values and social norms.

Libertarian conservatives advocate for minimal government interference in both the economic and social spheres. They believe in a free-market system where individuals and businesses can freely engage in voluntary transactions without excessive regulation or government intervention. They emphasize the importance of limited government power to safeguard individual rights and promote economic prosperity.

While sharing some common ground with libertarians, libertarian conservatives differ in their emphasis on preserving and promoting traditional values and institutions. They place importance on maintaining social order, upholding traditional family structures, and preserving cultural norms. They view these values as integral to the stability and well-being of society.

Libertarian conservatives may also emphasize the importance of personal responsibility and self-reliance, believing that individuals should be free to make their own choices and bear the consequences of their actions.

Neo

Neoconservatism is a political ideology that emerged in the United States during the late 20th century. It combines conservative principles with a proactive and interventionist approach to foreign policy. Neoconservatives advocate for the promotion of democracy, free markets, and American values on the global stage.

Neoconservatism originated from a group of intellectuals who had initially been associated with the political left but later shifted their focus to issues of national security and foreign policy. They became disillusioned with what they perceived as the failures of liberal policies, particularly in dealing with the challenges posed by the Soviet Union and communism.

Neoconservatives prioritize a strong and assertive military, believing that American power should be used to advance democracy and protect national security interests. They argue for a moral and value-driven foreign policy, asserting that promoting democracy and human rights abroad serves the long-term interests of the United States.

On domestic policy, neoconservatives tend to support free-market principles, emphasizing the importance of entrepreneurship, limited government regulation, and lower taxes. They also advocate for a strong stance on law and order issues, favoring tough criminal justice policies.

Paleo

Paleoconservatism is a political ideology that emerged in the United States in the late 20th century, emphasizing traditional conservative values and a skepticism toward rapid social and cultural change. Paleoconservatives advocate for limited government, constitutionalism, traditional social institutions, and a cautious approach to international interventionism.

Paleoconservatives draw inspiration from conservative thinkers such as Russell Kirk and Richard Weaver, who emphasized the importance of preserving tradition, cultural heritage, and the social fabric of society. They prioritize the preservation of local communities, traditional family structures, and religious values.

Paleoconservatives often express concerns about the erosion of national identity, the decline of moral values, and the influence of globalism and multiculturalism. They argue for immigration restrictions and cultural assimilation to protect the integrity and unity of the nation.

While sharing common ground with other strands of conservatism, paleoconservatives diverge from neoconservatism and libertarianism on certain issues. They reject the interventionist foreign policies associated with neoconservatism and advocate for a more restrained approach to international affairs. Paleoconservatives also criticize the free-market orientation of libertarianism and emphasize the need for government intervention to safeguard local communities and industries.

Paternalistic

Paternalistic conservatism is a political ideology that combines conservative principles with a belief in the responsibility of the state to protect and guide its citizens. It advocates for a strong and interventionist government that seeks to provide social welfare, maintain social order, and protect traditional values.

Paternalistic conservatives believe that society functions best when individuals adhere to certain moral and cultural norms. They see the state as a paternal figure that should protect its citizens from harm and ensure their well-being. This can manifest in policies such as social welfare programs, regulation of societal behaviors, and the promotion of traditional family structures.

While paternalistic conservatives value individual liberty, they also prioritize the stability and cohesion of society. They argue that a well-ordered society requires the guidance and direction provided by a strong central authority. Paternalistic conservatives often emphasize the importance of social hierarchy, authority, and tradition in maintaining social order and cohesion.

Progressive

Progressive conservatism combines conservative principles with a commitment to social progress and addressing social issues. It seeks to blend traditional conservative values with a recognition of the need for social and economic reform.

Progressive conservatives advocate for a balanced approach to governance, emphasizing the importance of both individual liberty and social responsibility. They support limited government intervention while recognizing that some societal problems require proactive measures and targeted policies to ensure equal opportunity and social justice.

Progressive conservatives often prioritize education, healthcare, and social welfare programs to address societal inequalities and promote upward mobility.

They believe in the importance of investing in social infrastructure and supporting marginalized communities to foster social cohesion and economic prosperity.

At the same time, progressive conservatives often uphold traditional values and cultural heritage. They value the stability and continuity provided by strong institutions and emphasize the importance of family, community, and social cohesion in promoting individual well-being and societal harmony.

Constitutional Monarchism

Constitutional monarchism is a political system in which a monarch, typically a king or queen, serves as the head of state, while the day to day governance and decision-making are carried out by an elected government operating under a constitution. This form of governance seeks to strike a balance between the traditional symbolism and historical continuity represented by the monarchy and the principles of democratic governance.

In a constitutional monarchy, the powers of the monarch are usually limited by a constitution or a set of laws, which outline the division of authority between the monarch and the elected representatives. The constitution often delineates the rights and responsibilities of both the monarch and the government, safeguarding individual liberties and setting the framework for the rule of law.

One of the primary advantages of constitutional monarchy is its ability to provide stability and continuity to a nation. The hereditary nature of the monarchy can foster a sense of national identity and tradition, while the constitutional framework ensures that the government remains accountable to the people.

Unlike absolute monarchies, where the monarch wields significant power and authority, constitutional monarchies typically have limited political influence. The monarch may serve as a ceremonial figurehead, representing the unity and history of the nation, without interfering in the day-to-day affairs of governance.

Countries with constitutional monarchies vary in the degree of power granted to the monarch. Some monarchs may play a more active role in ceremonial duties, diplomacy, or providing advice to the government, while others maintain a largely symbolic role.

Examples of countries with constitutional monarchies include the United Kingdom, Japan, Sweden, Canada, and many others. Each of these nations has its unique constitutional arrangements, reflecting the historical and cultural context in which their monarchy evolved.

Demarchy

Demarchy, also known as sortition or random selection, is a political system that proposes choosing public officials and decision-makers through a lottery or random process rather than by elections. It was present in Athens before the advent of democracy. In a demarchic system, citizens are selected at random to serve in various governing bodies, such as legislative assemblies or advisory councils. Advocates of demarchy argue that it promotes greater representation and participation, as it ensures that a diverse range of individuals from various backgrounds and experiences have the opportunity to serve in government. It is seen as a potential remedy to the issues of career politicians, electoral biases, and money-driven politics. However, demarchy also raises concerns about the qualifications and expertise of randomly selected officials and the potential for populism and manipulation.

Democracy

Democracy is a political ideology and system of governance that emphasizes the participation and representation of citizens in decision-making processes. Rooted in the principles of equality, freedom, and popular sovereignty, democracy aims to ensure that power is vested in the people and that their voices and interests are taken into account.

At its core, democracy rests on several key principles:

- Popular Sovereignty: Democracy asserts that ultimate authority resides in the people. The power to govern is derived from the consent of the governed, and political leaders are accountable to the citizens.

- Political Equality: Democracy advocates for equal political rights and opportunities for all citizens, regardless of their background, social status, or wealth. Each individual has an equal say in the decision-making process and the ability to participate in shaping public policy.

- Majority Rule and Minority Rights: Democracy respects the will of the majority while protecting the rights and interests of minority groups. This principle recognizes that while majority decisions should prevail, minority rights and viewpoints should be safeguarded and respected.

- Rule of Law: Democracy upholds the principle of rule of law, where laws are applied equally and consistently to all citizens, including those in positions of power. It ensures that no one is above the law and that the legal system provides a framework for fairness, justice, and protection of individual rights.

- Freedom of Expression and Assembly: Democracy values freedom of speech, press, and assembly as essential components of an informed and engaged citizenry. These freedoms allow individuals to voice their opinions, criticize the government, and peacefully assemble to express their grievances or advocate for change.

- Separation of Powers: Democracy often incorporates a system of checks and balances, where power is divided among different branches of government (such as the executive, legislative, and judicial branches) to prevent the concentration of power and to ensure accountability and transparency.

While democracy is an overarching concept, there are various forms and models that can be observed around the world. Some of the most common include:

- Representative Democracy: In representative democracy, citizens elect representatives to make decisions on their behalf. This form of democracy allows for efficient decision-making and representation of diverse interests, while also ensuring that elected officials are accountable to the electorate.

- Direct Democracy: Direct democracy emphasizes direct citizen participation in decision-making. This can take the form of referendums, town hall meetings, or citizen initiatives, where citizens have the ability to directly vote on specific issues or policies.

- Liberal Democracy: Liberal democracy combines the principles of democracy with a strong emphasis on individual rights, civil liberties, and the rule of law. Liberal democracies aim to protect individual freedoms while maintaining the core democratic principles of participation and representation.

Throughout history, democracy has evolved and expanded. It has been the catalyst for significant social and political movements, such as the civil rights movement, women's suffrage, and anti-colonialism. Democracy continues to be a dynamic and evolving ideology that adapts to the changing needs and aspirations of societies.

Dengism

Deng Xiaoping was a prominent Chinese revolutionary and statesman who played a pivotal role in shaping the ideology and policies of modern China. His ideology, often referred to as "Deng Xiaoping Theory," emerged in the late 20th century and laid the foundation for China's economic reforms and opening-up policy.

Deng Xiaoping's ideology emphasized pragmatic and market-oriented approaches to address China's economic and social challenges. He believed that socialism should adapt to the changing realities of a modernizing society, and he famously remarked, "It doesn't matter if a cat is black or white, as long as it catches mice."

Under Deng's leadership, China embarked on a series of economic reforms, introducing elements of market competition and private enterprise while retaining a one-party socialist system. His policies encouraged foreign investment and trade, leading to significant economic growth and the lifting of millions of people out of poverty.

Deng also advocated for a strong military and a policy of "peaceful coexistence" in foreign affairs, which helped China improve its global standing and open up to the international community.

While Deng Xiaoping's economic reforms were widely praised for their transformative impact on China's development, his legacy remains a topic of debate. Critics argue that his emphasis on economic growth and development came at the expense of political freedom and human rights. Nevertheless, Deng's ideology continues to shape China's political and economic trajectory, as the country remains a global economic powerhouse with significant geopolitical influence.

Distributism

Distributism is an economic and political ideology that emerged in the early 20th century as a response to the perceived ills of both capitalism and socialism. It advocates for the widespread distribution of property and the decentralization of economic power, aiming to create a more equitable and sustainable society.

At its core, distributism is grounded in the principles of Catholic social teaching and the belief in the dignity of the human person and the importance of the family as the fundamental unit of society. It seeks to promote a more balanced and just economic system by advocating for widespread property ownership and the diffusion of economic power among individuals and small-scale enterprises.

Distributism challenges the concentration of wealth and economic power that is often associated with both capitalism and socialism. It argues that the widespread ownership of productive property, such as land, farms, and small businesses, is essential for creating a more stable, prosperous, and morally sound society. Distributists believe that a wide distribution of property ensures economic independence, fosters local communities, and strengthens social bonds.

One of the key principles of distributism is the concept of subsidiarity, which emphasizes that decisions should be made at the most local level possible. Distributists argue that economic decision-making should occur at the level of the family, community, and small-scale enterprises, rather than being concentrated in the hands of large corporations or centralized government entities. This principle aims to empower individuals and promote a more participatory and democratic economic system.

Distributism also places a strong emphasis on the importance of sustainable and responsible stewardship of the environment. It rejects the exploitative nature of unrestrained capitalism and advocates for practices that are in harmony with nature and promote long-term ecological sustainability. Distributists believe that a more localized and decentralized economy can better prioritize environmental concerns and promote a more balanced relationship between humans and the natural world.

While distributism has influenced various movements and thinkers, its practical implementation has been limited. Some argue that distributism may face challenges in a globalized and interconnected world, where large-scale industries and multinational corporations dominate the economic landscape. Nonetheless, distributism continues to inspire discussions and debates about alternative economic systems that prioritize social justice, human dignity, and sustainability.

Dominionism

Dominionism is a broad term used to describe various Christian theological perspectives that advocate for Christians to have a significant influence over secular society. It posits that Christians have a divine mandate to exercise dominion or authority over all aspects of society, including politics, culture, education, and the economy. However, it is important to note that dominionism is not a monolithic ideology and encompasses a range of beliefs and interpretations.

Elective Monarchism

Elective monarchism is a political system in which the monarch is chosen through a process of election rather than inheriting the position based on a royal lineage or bloodline. In contrast to hereditary monarchies, where the crown passes from one generation to another, elective monarchies allow for the selection of a ruler from among eligible candidates.

In elective monarchies, the methods of choosing a monarch can vary widely. The process may involve an assembly of nobles, clergy, or representatives from various regions, who come together to deliberate and vote on the candidate they believe should become the new monarch. Alternatively, a council of influential figures or a specific group of people, such as a royal family or aristocracy, may have the authority to elect the monarch.

One of the key advantages of elective monarchism is that it allows for a degree of flexibility and adaptability in selecting a ruler. It can potentially lead to the election of a capable and qualified candidate, irrespective of their lineage, based on their merits and leadership abilities. This can help ensure that the best-suited person assumes the throne, which may not always be the case in hereditary monarchies where succession is predetermined.

However, elective monarchies can also present challenges and potential drawbacks. The process of electing a monarch may be prone to political maneuvering, factionalism, or external influences, leading to instability and uncertainty. Moreover, the lack of a clear line of succession could create power struggles and disputes among candidates and their supporters, potentially leading to civil strife.

Historically, elective monarchies were more common in various regions, especially during the Middle Ages and early modern period. The Holy Roman Empire and the Polish-Lithuanian Commonwealth are notable examples of historical elective monarchies.

Today, the vast majority of monarchies are hereditary, with the crown passing from one generation to the next within a specific royal family. However, the concept of elective monarchism continues to be of interest to some political thinkers and proponents of alternative governance models.

Overall, elective monarchism offers an alternative perspective on the role of monarchy in governance, allowing for the possibility of merit-based leadership selection. While it has been less prevalent in modern times, its historical significance and its potential to influence discussions on political legitimacy and leadership remain noteworthy.

Fascism

Italian Fascism

Introduction

Italian Fascism, sometimes known as Classical Fascism, inaugurated under the leadership of Benito Mussolini, emerged in the early 20th century as a distinctive political ideology that aimed to establish a totalitarian state. While rooted in nationalism and authoritarianism, Italian Fascism also incorporated elements of corporatism, anti-liberalism, and aggressive expansionism. In this article, we will delve into the core tenets, historical context, and lasting impact of Italian Fascism.

Origins and Historical Context

Italian Fascism emerged against the backdrop of social, economic, and political turmoil in post-World War I Italy. It sought to address the perceived weaknesses of liberal democracy and Marxism, offering a new vision of national rejuvenation and order. Mussolini capitalized on nationalistic sentiments, a desire for strong leadership, and a discontent with the perceived failures of the democratic system to rally support for his fascist movement.

Authoritarian Nationalism and the Cult of the Leader

Italian Fascism emphasized the primacy of the nation and the need for a strong, centralized state. Nationalism was a key component of the ideology, promoting national unity, pride, and expansion. The cult of the leader played a significant role, with Mussolini projecting himself as the embodiment of the nation's destiny and as the charismatic figure who could lead Italy to greatness. The authoritarian nature of Italian Fascism subordinated individual liberties and freedoms to the interests of the state.

Corporatism and Suppression of Political Dissent

Italian Fascism advocated for the incorporation of different societal groups into a corporatist system, in which labor unions, employers, and professional organizations were organized under the control of the state. This model aimed to suppress class conflict and create a harmonious society, albeit one under strict state control. However, in practice, this corporatist system often favored the interests of the ruling elite, stifling independent worker representation and dissent.

Imperialism and Expansionism

Italian Fascism pursued an aggressive foreign policy with aspirations of reviving the glory of the Roman Empire. Mussolini sought to expand Italian influence in the Mediterranean region and Africa through military conquests. The invasion of Ethiopia in 1935 and the occupation of Albania in 1939 were among the notable examples of Italian Fascist expansionism. This imperialist ambition aimed to solidify Mussolini's domestic support base and project Italian power on the world stage.

Racial Supremacy and Fascist Propaganda

Italian Fascism incorporated elements of racial supremacism, although to a lesser extent compared to Nazi Germany. Fascist propaganda promoted the idea of an Italian racial and cultural superiority, often presenting Italians as the heirs of the Roman civilization. However, Italian Fascism did not implement systematic genocide or persecution on the scale witnessed in Nazi Germany.

Legacy and Critiques

The legacy of Italian Fascism is deeply tarnished by its association with authoritarianism, political repression, and alliances with Nazi Germany during World War II. The fascist regime's support for dictatorships, its suppression of political opposition, and its aggressive foreign policy have left a lasting stain on Italian history. In the aftermath of World War II, the ideology was discredited and banned in Italy. However, it is essential to note that the impact of Fascism extended beyond Italy, influencing various far-right and nationalist movements around the world.

Nazism

Introduction

Nazism, also known as National Socialism, was a political ideology that emerged in Germany during the 20th century. Led by Adolf Hitler and the Nazi Party, Nazism combined elements of fascism, racial supremacy, and anti-Semitism.

Historical Context

The rise of Nazism was fueled by the social, economic, and political unrest following World War I. Germany faced economic hardships, political instability, and a sense of humiliation due to the Treaty of Versailles. These factors, combined with widespread discontent, created fertile ground for the emergence of radical ideologies like Nazism.

The Ideology of Nazism

Nazism was characterized by its extreme nationalism, totalitarianism, and racial ideology. It sought to establish a racially homogeneous and authoritarian state, viewing the Aryan race as superior and promoting the exclusion and persecution of those deemed racially inferior, particularly Jews. Central to Nazism was the notion of Lebensraum, or living space, which entailed territorial expansion to accommodate the perceived needs of the Germanic people.

At the core of Nazism was the concept of Aryan supremacy. The Nazis believed in the superiority of the "Aryan" race, which they considered to be a pure, Nordic lineage. This belief was heavily influenced by ideas of eugenics, which aimed to improve the genetic quality of the population through selective breeding and sterilization. Eugenic policies were implemented to enforce racial purity and eliminate what the Nazis deemed as undesirable traits from the population.

Hitler and Mein Kampf

Mein Kampf expounds Hitler's fervent nationalism and belief in the racial superiority of the Aryan race. Hitler idealized the German nation and emphasized the need to unite all Germans under one state, achieving self-sufficiency and military strength. He propagated the concept of Aryan racial supremacy, which he claimed as the foundation of German greatness and advocated for the elimination of other races deemed inferior.

A central theme in Mein Kampf is Hitler's intense anti-Semitism. He propagated a conspiracy theory, blaming Jews for various perceived societal ills and presenting them as a threat to the German nation. Hitler portrayed Jews as a race that corrupted culture, economy, and politics, further cementing their persecution and eventual extermination as a fundamental goal of the Nazi regime.

Hitler outlined his vision of acquiring Lebensraum, or living space, for the Aryan race in Mein Kampf. He believed that Germany needed to expand its territory to accommodate its growing population and ensure its economic and military dominance. Hitler's expansionist aspirations were particularly focused on the East, as he envisioned acquiring territories in Eastern Europe for German colonization and resources.

In Mein Kampf, Hitler expressed his disdain for liberal democracy and championed the idea of a totalitarian state. He believed in the supremacy of a single, strong leader who would possess absolute power. Hitler envisioned a hierarchical society with strict control over all aspects of life, including politics, culture, and education, to ensure the complete loyalty and obedience of the German people.

Hitler emphasized the importance of propaganda and indoctrination in Mein Kampf. He recognized the power of manipulating public opinion and believed in the necessity of creating a "new man" who would fully embrace Nazi ideology. Hitler sought to control education, media, and cultural institutions to shape the minds of the German population and promote unquestioning loyalty to the Nazi cause.

Alfred Rosenberg and his Influence

Alfred Rosenberg was a Nazi ideologue and a key figure in shaping the intellectual foundations of Nazism. As the head of the Office of Foreign Affairs and later the Reich Ministry for the Occupied Eastern Territories, Rosenberg played a significant role in disseminating Nazi ideology during the Nazi regime. His work, "The Myth of the Twentieth Century," exerted a profound impact on Nazi ideology, particularly in the realm of racial and cultural theories.

Rosenberg's "The Myth of the Twentieth Century" presented a novel interpretation of history, emphasizing the primacy of the Aryan race and the need to eradicate perceived racial and cultural threats. His writings propagated the notion of a grand racial struggle and the necessity of reclaiming Germanic dominance. Rosenberg's ideas heavily influenced the Nazi party's policies on race, culture, and expansion.

Rosenberg's theories on racial and cultural supremacy played a significant role in shaping Nazi ideology. He argued for the preservation and advancement of Germanic racial purity, condemning racial mixing and considering non-Aryan races as threats to the Germanic people. Rosenberg's writings provided a pseudo-intellectual justification for the Nazi party's policies of racial exclusion, discrimination, and persecution.

Rosenberg's writings also contributed to the pervasive anti-Semitism within Nazi ideology. He propagated the belief in a worldwide Jewish conspiracy, attributing the perceived decline of German society and the threat to Aryan purity to Jewish influence. Rosenberg's ideas further fueled the anti-Semitic sentiment already prevalent in Germany, providing intellectual backing for the Nazi regime's systematic persecution and genocide of Jews.

Rosenberg's ideas were influential in shaping Nazi policies, particularly in the realms of racial ideology, culture, and education. He championed the suppression of "degenerate" art and advocated for the promotion of Nazi-approved cultural expressions. Rosenberg's influence extended to the occupation of Eastern territories, where his racist theories were applied to justify brutal policies and the exploitation of conquered peoples.

While Rosenberg's ideas played a significant role in Nazi ideology, it is crucial to note that they were not universally accepted within the Nazi Party. Some party members, including Hitler himself, did not fully embrace Rosenberg's theories, and there were disagreements among Nazi leaders on certain aspects of his ideas. However, despite internal differences, Rosenberg's influence on Nazi policies cannot be disregarded.

Austria

Austro-fascism was a distinct form of fascism that emerged in Austria during the interwar period in the 1930s. Though a direct influence is not certain, it bore some resemblance to the corporate statist system proposed by Othmar Spann. While it shared similarities with its Italian and German counterparts, several factors made Austrian fascism unique. In fact, the labeling of "Austro-fascism" as fascist has been disputed, with some contending that the Austrian government of this period is more properly described as authoritarian conservative rather than fascist.

One of the key factors was its origin and development within a specific historical context. After World War I and the dissolution of the Austro-Hungarian Empire, Austria became a young republic struggling with economic instability, political polarization, and rising social tensions. Amid these challenges, the authoritarian and nationalist ideas of fascism found fertile ground.

Another factor that set Austro-fascism apart was its pragmatic approach to nationalism. Austrian fascists, led by Engelbert Dollfuss and later Kurt Schuschnigg, sought to promote a sense of Austrian national identity while preserving the idea of a separate Austrian state. They emphasized Austrian exceptionalism and sought to distance themselves from both Germany and Italy, even as they drew inspiration from some aspects of Italian fascism.

Additionally, Austro-fascism incorporated elements of corporatism, aiming to create a harmonious and hierarchical society in which labor, industry, and the state collaborated to achieve national unity and economic stability. This corporatist model differed from the more aggressive and militaristic style of the German Nazis.

Austro-fascism also faced a unique challenge concerning its relationship with the Catholic Church. The regime sought to maintain the Church's support while asserting its own authority over matters of state, which led to complex negotiations and compromises between the two.

Despite its unique features, Austro-fascism ultimately faced internal divisions and opposition, particularly from socialist and communist groups. In 1938, Nazi Germany annexed Austria in the Anschluss, bringing an end to Austro-fascism and incorporating the country into the Third Reich.

Britain

British fascism, as embodied by Sir Oswald Mosley, was a political ideology that emerged in the early 20th century and sought to establish an authoritarian and corporatist state in Britain. Oswald Mosley, a former member of the Conservative Party and later a Labour MP, founded the British Union of Fascists (BUF) in 1932.

Mosley's ideology was influenced by the fascist movements that emerged in Europe during the interwar period, particularly Benito Mussolini's Italy. He espoused a vision of strong leadership, nationalism, and a rejection of parliamentary democracy in favor of a single-party system.

The BUF attracted support from various sections of British society, including disgruntled veterans, middle-class intellectuals, and some members of the working class who were dissatisfied with the economic hardships of the time. However, it also faced strong opposition from the government, other political parties, and anti-fascist groups.

The BUF's tactics, such as the use of paramilitary uniforms and street demonstrations, often led to violent clashes with anti-fascist protesters. In response, the government enacted legislation, such as the Public Order Act of 1936, to restrict the activities of the BUF and other groups.

The outbreak of World War II and the prospect of conflict with Nazi Germany further discredited British fascism and led to the internment of Mosley and other prominent members of the BUF under the Defense Regulation 18B. After the war, Mosley's political influence waned, and he remained a controversial figure until his death in 1980.

Spain

Falangism, also known as Spanish Fascism, was a political ideology that emerged in Spain during the 1930s. It was founded by José Antonio Primo de Rivera in 1933, inspired by the fascist movements of Italy and Germany. Falangism played a significant role during the Spanish Civil War (1936-1939) and became the ideological foundation of Francisco Franco's regime.

Falangism emphasized authoritarianism, nationalism, and anti-communism. It sought to create a centralized, corporatist state that would unify the Spanish nation and suppress regional identities. The ideology exalted the values of discipline, hierarchy, and duty, rejecting individualism and promoting the idea of collective identity above personal interests.

Falangism incorporated traditional Catholic elements and sought to maintain close ties with the Catholic Church. It envisioned the church as an essential pillar of the state, reinforcing conservative social values and reinforcing the regime's authority.

During the Spanish Civil War, the Falange Española Tradicionalista y de las Juntas de Ofensiva Nacional Sindicalista (FET y de las JONS) became the ruling party, joining forces with other right-wing factions supporting Franco's Nationalist forces. However, over time, Franco's regime began to distance itself from some of the more radical elements of the Falange, instead consolidating power under Franco's military-led authoritarian rule.

Under Franco's rule, Falangism was gradually incorporated into the broader nationalist and authoritarian framework of Francoism, losing some of its distinctive features. After Franco's death in 1975 and the transition to democracy, the Falange party declined in influence and significance. Today, Falangism remains a historically significant chapter in Spanish political history, but the ideology's impact has diminished, and it is no longer a dominant force in contemporary Spanish politics.

Romania

The Romanian Iron Guard, also known as "Garda de Fier" in Romanian, was a far-right and ultranationalist political movement that emerged in Romania during the 1930s. Founded by Corneliu Zelea Codreanu in 1927, the Iron Guard sought to establish an authoritarian and fascist state based on an extreme form of Romanian nationalism and Orthodox Christianity.

At its core, the ideology of the Iron Guard emphasized the rejection of liberal democracy, parliamentary politics, and the perceived corrupt elites. Instead, it promoted a vision of an organic, spiritual, and ethnically pure Romania, seeking to create a national community unified by shared values and traditions.

The movement's emblem, a triple cross resembling a swastika, reflected its commitment to religious symbolism and radical nationalism. The Iron Guard propagated the idea of a "Legionary State" led by a single "Captain," embodying a blend of political leader and spiritual guide.

The Iron Guard attracted a significant following, especially among disaffected youths and rural communities, who were disillusioned with the existing political establishment and the country's socioeconomic conditions. Their paramilitary activities and confrontations with political rivals, especially the left-wing and Jewish communities, led to growing tensions and violence in Romanian society.

However, despite its popularity, the Iron Guard faced opposition from King Carol II, who viewed it as a threat to the monarchy and the stability of the country. In 1938, Carol II dissolved the Iron Guard and established a royal dictatorship. Following a failed coup attempt, the Iron Guard was officially banned in 1939.

The legacy of the Iron Guard remains controversial and divisive in Romania's history. Some see it as a precursor to later fascist movements, while others condemn its violent methods and extremist ideology. Today, Romania has embraced a democratic system, but the legacy of the Iron Guard continues to be a subject of study and debate.

Federalism

Federalism is a political ideology and system of government that emphasizes the distribution of power between a central authority and its constituent units, typically states or provinces. In a federal system, the central government coexists with regional or local governments, each possessing their own distinct powers and responsibilities as outlined in a constitution or a set of laws.

The key principle of federalism is that it allows for the division of authority, granting certain powers to the central government while reserving others for the regional governments. This division of powers helps to strike a balance between national unity and local autonomy, enabling different regions or states to have some degree of self-governance while remaining part of a larger political entity.

One of the main advantages of federalism is that it accommodates diversity within a country, allowing regions with distinct cultures, languages, or historical backgrounds to retain some degree of control over their affairs. This setup is particularly valuable in large and culturally diverse nations, as it helps prevent the concentration of power in a single centralized authority and promotes a sense of belonging and ownership among citizens.

Federalist Party (United States)

The Federalist Party was one of the first political parties in the United States, founded in the 1790s by Alexander Hamilton, John Adams, and other prominent figures. It stood in opposition to the Democratic-Republican Party led by Thomas Jefferson and James Madison. The Federalists advocated for a strong federal government, a strong national economy, and a loose interpretation of the U.S. Constitution.

Alexander Hamilton and his supporters, often referred to as the "High Federalists," were the driving force behind the party's economic policies. They believed in a centralized government with significant powers to promote economic growth and establish a strong national financial system. Hamilton's economic plan included the assumption of state debts, the creation of a national bank, and the imposition of tariffs to protect domestic industries. They favored close ties with Britain and a pro-British foreign policy.

On the other hand, the supporters of John Adams, the second President of the United States, represented a more moderate faction within the Federalist Party. They were referred to as "Adams Federalists." While they agreed with the need for a strong federal government, they were less enthusiastic about some of Hamilton's more ambitious proposals, such as a large standing army and a powerful central bank. The Adams Federalists focused on diplomacy and sought to avoid conflicts with both Britain and France during their ongoing war.

The Federalist Party's ideology also involved a loose interpretation of the U.S. Constitution, allowing for a broader interpretation of federal powers when necessary to achieve the country's goals. They believed that the federal government should possess the authority to take actions not explicitly stated in the Constitution if deemed necessary for the country's well-being and prosperity.

The Federalist Party eventually faced opposition from the Democratic-Republican Party, led by Thomas Jefferson, and gradually lost support. By the early 19th century, the party's influence waned, leading to its decline and eventual dissolution. Nonetheless, the Federalists' legacy remains significant, as their ideas on a strong federal government and economic policies have had a lasting impact on the development of the United States.

Feminism

Feminism is a multifaceted social and political ideology that advocates for gender equality and the recognition of women's rights. At its core, feminism seeks to challenge and dismantle perceived inequalities and discrimination based on gender, aiming to create a more just and equitable society for all individuals, regardless of their gender identity.

The history of feminism dates back to the 19th and early 20th centuries when suffragettes fought for women's right to vote and expanded to address a wide range of gender-related issues. Feminist movements have evolved over time and encompass diverse perspectives and approaches, reflecting the unique experiences and challenges faced by women worldwide.

Feminists work towards breaking down gender norms and stereotypes, promoting women's empowerment, and advocating for policies and practices that advance gender equality in areas such as education, the workplace, healthcare, and representation in politics and leadership roles.

Moreover, feminism is not solely concerned with women's rights but also recognizes the interconnectedness of gender issues with other social identities, including race, class, sexuality, and ability. Intersectional feminism, an important branch of the movement, acknowledges and addresses the intersecting forms of discrimination and oppression experienced by individuals with multiple marginalized identities.

Francoism

Francoism refers to the political ideology and authoritarian rule of General Francisco Franco in Spain from 1939 to his death in 1975. Following the Spanish Civil War, Franco emerged victorious, establishing a dictatorship that sought to impose his vision of a centralized, nationalist, and traditionalist Spain.

Francoism was characterized by its rejection of liberal democracy, communism, and regional autonomy. Instead, it promoted a strong, centralized state with Franco as the head of state and government. The regime emphasized the principles of Catholicism, anti-communism, and Spanish nationalism. Franco's government suppressed political opposition, censored the media, and curtailed individual freedoms to maintain strict control over society.

Economically, Francoism adopted a corporatist model, bringing together the state, labor unions, and business interests under its control. The regime pursued a policy of economic autarky, limiting foreign trade and investment, which led to economic stagnation and isolation from the international community.

During Franco's rule, Spain experienced relative stability, particularly after the early years of repression and conflict. However, the regime's human rights abuses and lack of political freedoms were widely criticized by the international community.

Following Franco's death in 1975, Spain transitioned to a democratic system, leading to the adoption of a new constitution in 1978. This marked the end of Francoism and the beginning of Spain's modern democratic era. Today, Francoism remains a contentious chapter in Spanish history, with debates continuing about its legacy and impact on the country's political and social development.

Gaddafism

Muammar Gaddafi, the de facto leader of Libya from 1969 until his death in 2011, developed a unique political ideology known as "The Third International Theory" or "The Green Book." Gaddafi's ideology was an amalgamation of Arab nationalism, socialism, and Islamic principles, often referred to as "Gaddafi's Third Way."

At the heart of Gaddafi's ideology was his rejection of Western-style democracy and capitalism. He criticized representative democracy as a system of exploitation, advocating instead for direct democracy through popular committees and people's congresses. Gaddafi argued that these bodies would ensure genuine participation and decision-making by the Libyan people, though in practice, they were largely controlled by his regime.

Economic principles under Gaddafi's ideology revolved around his vision of a state-centered socialist economy. The government nationalized key industries and resources, seeking to redistribute wealth and provide free education, healthcare, and welfare services to Libyan citizens. Gaddafi also sought to eliminate class distinctions and promote social equality through the establishment of people's committees that were supposed to govern local communities.

Gaddafi's ideology was also marked by pan-African aspirations, aiming to unite African nations politically and economically. He advocated for a United States of Africa as a means to combat neocolonialism and promote African self-sufficiency.

Ultimately, Gaddafi's ideology and leadership faced significant challenges, leading to internal dissent and opposition. In 2011, the Arab Spring protests erupted in Libya, demanding political reforms and an end to Gaddafi's rule. The situation escalated into a civil war, and Gaddafi's regime was eventually overthrown with the intervention of NATO forces. Gaddafi was killed in October 2011, bringing an end to his controversial political ideology and leadership in Libya.

Georgism

Georgism, named after the American economist and social reformer Henry George (1839-1897), is an economic and social ideology that centers around the concept of land value taxation. It proposes that land and natural resources belong to all members of society collectively rather than being subject to private ownership.

At the core of Georgism is the idea that land is a unique factor of production, and its value is created by the community and natural processes rather than individual effort. Georgists argue that land should be treated as a common resource, and its value should be collected through a tax known as the "single tax" or "land value tax."

The single tax is based on the unimproved value of land, excluding any improvements made by individuals, such as buildings or crops. By implementing this tax, Georgists believe that it would not only provide a fair and just revenue source for the government but also discourage land speculation and underutilization, leading to more efficient land use.

Moreover, Georgists contend that land value taxation could reduce wealth inequality and provide a more equitable distribution of wealth since land values often accrue to landowners without their direct effort.

Henry George's influential book, "Progress and Poverty," published in 1879, became a seminal work in the Georgist movement. The ideology gained traction in various parts of the world, particularly in the late 19th and early 20th centuries, and influenced numerous social and economic reform movements.

While Georgism remains a relatively niche ideology, its core principles of land value taxation and economic justice continue to be discussed and debated by economists, policymakers, and social activists seeking alternative approaches to address issues of poverty, inequality, and sustainable resource management.

Girondism

Girondism was a political ideology and a faction during the French Revolution in the late 18th century. The Girondists were moderate republicans who advocated for a constitutional monarchy and represented the interests of the provincial middle class. They derived their name from the department of Gironde in southwestern France, where many of their leaders hailed from.

The Girondists believed in limited government intervention and individual liberties, promoting a vision of a decentralized and federalist France. They supported free-market policies and were in favor of economic liberalism, seeking to promote commerce, trade, and private property rights.

While they supported the ideals of the French Revolution, such as equality before the law and the abolition of feudal privileges, the Girondists were cautious about the radical actions proposed by the more radical Jacobin faction.

They opposed the execution of King Louis XVI and sought a more peaceful resolution to the ongoing conflicts with foreign powers.

However, despite their moderate stance, the Girondists faced challenges from both the radical Jacobins and the more conservative elements of society. As the Revolution intensified and the Reign of Terror began, the Girondists lost influence, and many of their leaders were arrested and executed.

The fall of the Girondists marked a turning point in the French Revolution, as the radical Jacobins took control and initiated a more radical and centralized form of government. The Reign of Terror, under the leadership of Maximilien Robespierre, led to the execution of thousands of perceived enemies of the Revolution, including many former Girondist leaders.

In retrospect, Girondism is seen as a moderate and pragmatic political ideology that sought to balance revolutionary ideals with the need for stability and order. While they ultimately lost the power struggle during the Revolution, the Girondists left a lasting impact on the development of political thought and democratic principles in France and beyond.

Globalism

Globalism is an ideology that emphasizes interconnectedness, cooperation, and integration on a global scale. It promotes the idea of a unified and interdependent world, where nations, economies, cultures, and societies are increasingly linked and interwoven. Globalists advocate for the removal of barriers to trade, investment, and communication, fostering a global community that transcends national borders. They believe that collective action and collaboration among nations are essential for addressing global challenges such as climate change, poverty, and pandemics. However, globalism also faces criticism from those who argue that it can lead to the erosion of national sovereignty and local cultures, and may prioritize the interests of multinational corporations over those of individual nations and their citizens. As globalization continues to shape the modern world, the debate over the merits and drawbacks of globalism is likely to persist.

High Toryism

High Toryism, also known as Tory Corporatism, is a political ideology that emerged in Britain during the late 17th and early 18th centuries. It represents a traditionalist and conservative approach to governance, emphasizing the preservation of established institutions, social hierarchies, and traditional values.

High Tories were ardent defenders of the monarchy, the Church of England, and the aristocracy. They believed in the divine right of kings, asserting that the monarch's authority was derived from God, and they sought to maintain the privileges and influence of the nobility as the bedrock of social order.

At the heart of High Toryism was the idea that society should be organized into organic hierarchical structures, where each individual and social group had a distinct role and responsibility. They viewed society as an interconnected whole, with each part contributing to the stability and well-being of the entire nation.

Economically, High Tories favored a form of corporatism, where the government played a role in regulating the economy and mediating between labor, business, and other interest groups. They believed that economic activities should be coordinated and directed in the service of the common good and national interest, rather than being solely driven by individual self-interest and the pursuit of profit.

High Tories were critical of radical Enlightenment ideas and the concept of universal rights, which they saw as undermining traditional authority and social order. Instead, they stressed the importance of duty, loyalty, and adherence to traditional values and customs.

Over time, the influence of High Toryism waned as Britain underwent significant social, economic, and political transformations. The rise of classical liberalism, industrialization, and urbanization brought about a shift towards more progressive and market-oriented policies.

Today, the principles of High Toryism continue to resonate with some conservative thinkers and traditionalists who advocate for the preservation of cultural heritage, social stability, and a more interventionist approach to governance. However, in modern political discourse, Tory Corporatism is not as prominent as other forms of conservatism.

Integralism

Integralism emerged in the early 20th century, particularly in Brazil, and was influenced by both conservative and fascist ideas. It sought to create a centralized and corporatist state with strong ties to the Catholic Church. Integralists believed in the unity of all social classes and aimed to eliminate class struggle through a hierarchical social structure. They rejected individualism and sought to prioritize the collective interests of the nation.

Integralism emphasized the importance of national identity, traditional values, and a rejection of liberal democracy. It viewed the state as the ultimate authority and defended the idea of a strong leader to guide the nation.

The most prominent integralist movement was the Brazilian Integralist Action, founded in 1932 by Plínio Salgado. While it gained considerable popularity during the 1930s, its support declined following political repression and the outbreak of World War II. The Brazilian Integralist Action was dissolved in 1938, but its influence lingered in some right-wing circles.

Islamism

Islamism is a political ideology that seeks to establish Islamic principles and values as the foundation of governance and societal organization. It emerged in the 20th century as a response to the challenges faced by Muslim-majority countries in the modern world and their desire to preserve and promote their Islamic identity and heritage.

At its core, Islamism advocates for the implementation of Sharia, or Islamic law, as the guiding legal framework in the political, social, and legal spheres. Islamists believe that the application of Islamic teachings in all aspects of life will lead to a just and morally upright society.

Islamism encompasses a wide range of ideologies, from moderate and reformist approaches to more radical and militant expressions. Moderate Islamists often participate in democratic processes and seek to achieve their goals through peaceful means, focusing on social and political reforms. They aim to create societies where Islamic values coexist with democratic governance and human rights.

On the other hand, radical Islamists or jihadist groups advocate for a more militant approach, often resorting to violence and armed struggle to achieve their objectives. They reject existing political structures and advocate for the establishment of an Islamic state governed by their interpretation of Sharia.

Islamism gained significant attention in the late 20th and early 21st centuries, with the rise of various Islamist movements and parties in Muslim-majority countries. Some of the most notable examples include the Muslim Brotherhood in Egypt, Ennahda in Tunisia, and the AK Party in Turkey.

Jacksonian Democracy

Jacksonian Democracy refers to the political ideology and movement that emerged during the presidency of Andrew Jackson in the United States during the 1820s and 1830s. It was characterized by a commitment to expanding democratic participation, empowering the common man, and challenging the influence of established elites.

At the heart of Jacksonian Democracy was the belief in the inherent wisdom and virtue of the common people. Jacksonians advocated for broader suffrage, including the extension of voting rights to white males without property qualifications. They argued that political power should be vested in the hands of ordinary citizens rather than limited to a select aristocratic class.

One of the defining features of Jacksonian Democracy was its opposition to concentrated economic and political power. Jacksonians viewed the Second Bank of the United States as an embodiment of privilege and corruption, leading to its eventual dismantling by President Jackson. They also criticized monopolies and sought to promote economic opportunities for the masses.

Jacksonian Democracy was also known for its emphasis on territorial expansion and westward expansion. Jacksonian leaders pursued policies that facilitated the relocation and removal of Native American tribes from their ancestral lands to open up more territory for white settlers.

Jacobinism

The Jacobins were a radical political faction during the French Revolution, named after the Dominican convent in Paris where they held their meetings. Active from 1789 to 1794, the Jacobins played a crucial role in shaping the course of the Revolution and promoting a radical transformation of French society.

The Jacobin ideology was rooted in the principles of liberty, equality, and fraternity. They were ardent supporters of republicanism and advocated for the abolition of the monarchy, the establishment of a democratic government, and the empowerment of the common people. Their vision for society centered on the idea of a virtuous and unified nation, where all citizens were equal before the law and had the right to participate in politics.

Led by figures such as Maximilien Robespierre, Georges Danton, and Jean-Paul Marat, the Jacobins championed social and political reforms that aimed to eradicate the remnants of feudalism and aristocracy. They promoted measures such as the redistribution of land, the elimination of noble privileges, and the separation of church and state.

However, as the Revolution progressed, the Jacobins' ideology became more radical and authoritarian. They launched the Reign of Terror, a period of intense political repression and mass executions targeting perceived enemies of the Revolution. The Committee of Public Safety, led by Robespierre, assumed extraordinary powers to suppress dissent and safeguard the Revolution.

The Jacobins' increasing use of violence and their efforts to centralize power led to internal divisions and opposition from other factions. In 1794, the Thermidorian Reaction resulted in the downfall of the Jacobins, and Robespierre himself was executed, marking the end of their dominance in the French Revolution.

Jacobitism

Jacobitism was a political movement in Britain and Ireland that sought to restore the Catholic Stuart dynasty to the thrones of England, Scotland, and Ireland. The movement emerged in the late 17th century and was named after "Jacobus," the Latin form of James, the traditional name of the Stuart monarchs.

Jacobitism gained traction after the Glorious Revolution of 1688, when James II, a Catholic, was deposed and replaced by his Protestant daughter Mary and her husband, William of Orange. Many Catholics and some Protestants who remained loyal to the Stuart cause saw James II and his descendants as the legitimate rulers, believing in the doctrine of the divine right of kings.

Throughout the 18th century, Jacobitism became a symbol of opposition to the Hanoverian dynasty, which succeeded the Stuarts and held the British throne. Jacobite uprisings, notably in 1715 and 1745, attempted to restore the Stuart monarchy but ultimately failed.

Jacobitism had a romantic and nostalgic appeal, with many seeing the Stuart claimants as representing a return to a more traditional and unified Britain. The movement also had support in Scotland and Ireland, where grievances against the Hanoverian rule and religious tensions fueled its popularity.

Jeffersonian Democracy

Jeffersonian Democracy, also known as Jeffersonian Republicanism, is a political ideology and movement associated with Thomas Jefferson, the third President of the United States. It emerged during the late 18th and early 19th centuries and played a significant role in shaping the early American political landscape.

At its core, Jeffersonian Democracy emphasized agrarianism, states' rights, limited government, and individual liberty. Jeffersonians believed in the virtue of the yeoman farmer, viewing an independent, self-sufficient agrarian society as the ideal model for the nation. They were skeptical of urbanization, industrialization, and concentrated wealth, fearing that they could lead to the emergence of privileged elites and undermine the democratic ideals of the young republic.

Jeffersonian Republicans advocated for a strict interpretation of the U.S. Constitution, arguing that the federal government should be limited to its enumerated powers, with all other powers reserved to the states and the people. They were cautious about the expansion of federal authority, believing that it could threaten individual liberties and the sovereignty of the states.

Another key aspect of Jeffersonian Democracy was its opposition to a strong central banking system. Jefferson and his followers were deeply critical of the First Bank of the United States, arguing that it favored the interests of a wealthy few at the expense of ordinary citizens. They believed that the power to issue currency and regulate finances should remain with individual states and not be concentrated in a national bank.

Furthermore, Jeffersonian Republicans advocated for a non-interventionist foreign policy, promoting peaceful relations with other nations and avoiding entangling alliances. They prioritized the expansion of the United States' territory through the Louisiana Purchase, seeking to secure more land for agrarian settlement and westward expansion.

Jeffersonian Democracy's influence extended beyond Jefferson's presidency, leaving a lasting impact on American political thought. Despite the eventual demise of the Democratic-Republican Party, its ideas and principles continue to resonate with various political movements throughout American history, reflecting a commitment to limited government, individual freedom, and the preservation of states' rights.

Liberalism

Liberalism is a political and philosophical ideology that places a strong emphasis on individual freedom, equality, and the protection of individual rights. Rooted in the Enlightenment era, liberalism emerged as a response to authoritarian rule and the desire to establish a society based on reason, progress, and human autonomy. It champions the principles of limited government, the rule of law, free markets, and individual liberty as fundamental pillars of a just and prosperous society.

At the core of liberalism is the belief in the inherent worth and dignity of every individual. Liberals argue that individuals possess certain inalienable rights, such as freedom of speech, assembly, and religion, which should be protected by the state. They emphasize the importance of individual autonomy and the ability to pursue one's own goals and aspirations without undue interference from the government or other external forces.

Liberalism also promotes the concept of a social contract, where citizens voluntarily enter into an agreement with the government to secure their rights and provide for the common good. Liberals contend that the government's role should be limited to protecting these rights, maintaining law and order, and providing essential public services, while also fostering conditions for economic growth and individual opportunity.

Economically, liberalism embraces the principles of free markets and private property. Liberals argue that market competition leads to innovation, efficiency, and economic growth, benefiting society as a whole. They advocate for minimal government intervention in the economy, favoring deregulation and free trade. However, many liberals also recognize a need for social safety nets and welfare programs to provide a basic level of support and mitigate the negative effects of market forces on vulnerable individuals and communities.

Liberalism has evolved and diversified over time, giving rise to different strands within the ideology. Classical liberalism, associated with thinkers like John Locke and Adam Smith, focuses on limited government, individual liberty, and laissez-faire economics. Modern liberalism, also known as social liberalism, emphasizes the need for an active government role in addressing social and economic inequalities and ensuring a fair and just society.

Critics of liberalism argue that its emphasis on individualism and free markets can lead to social fragmentation and economic inequality. They contend that liberal policies may neglect the collective well-being and fail to address systemic issues such as poverty, discrimination, and environmental degradation. Some critics also argue that liberalism can prioritize individual rights over community values and cultural traditions. Nonetheless, liberalism remains one of the dominant political ideologies in many democratic societies around the world.

Classical

Classical liberalism, also known as laissez-faire liberalism, is a strand of liberalism that emerged during the Enlightenment and laid the foundation for many of the core principles of liberal thought. It places a strong emphasis on individual liberty, limited government, and free markets.

One of the central tenets of classical liberalism is the belief in individual freedom and autonomy. It asserts that individuals have the right to make their own choices, pursue their own interests, and engage in voluntary transactions without interference from the state. Classical liberals argue that government intervention in personal and economic affairs should be minimal, as it can infringe upon individual rights and stifle individual initiative and innovation.

Classical liberals advocate for limited government, which is constrained by a constitution or a set of fundamental laws. They argue that a smaller, less intrusive state is more conducive to preserving individual freedom and preventing the concentration of power. The role of the government, according to classical liberals, is primarily to protect individual rights, maintain law and order, and provide for national defense.

In terms of economic policy, classical liberals champion the virtues of free markets and private property. They contend that economic liberty and voluntary exchange are essential for economic growth, prosperity, and the efficient allocation of resources. They argue that government regulations and interventions in the economy, such as price controls and excessive taxation, hinder market mechanisms and impede economic progress.

Moreover, classical liberals argue that private property rights are a fundamental aspect of individual liberty. They believe that individuals have the right to own and control property, and that this ownership encourages responsible stewardship, incentivizes productivity, and allows for the accumulation of wealth.

However, it is important to note that classical liberalism does not reject the notion of a safety net entirely. While classical liberals emphasize limited government intervention, they acknowledge the need for some level of social assistance and support for the most vulnerable members of society. However, they generally prefer private philanthropy and voluntary initiatives over state-led welfare programs.

Conservative

Conservative liberalism is a political ideology that combines elements of both liberalism and conservatism. It seeks to reconcile the principles of individual freedom and limited government with a cautious and gradual approach to societal change and the preservation of traditional institutions and values.

Conservative liberals uphold the core principles of classical liberalism, including individual liberty, free markets, and limited government intervention. They advocate for the protection of individual rights and the belief that individuals should be free to pursue their own goals and interests without excessive state interference. Conservative liberals emphasize the importance of personal responsibility, self-reliance, and voluntary exchange in the marketplace.

However, conservative liberals also recognize the value of tradition, stability, and social cohesion. They argue that established institutions, customs, and cultural norms contribute to social order and provide a sense of continuity and identity. They believe that societal change should be gradual and respect the wisdom of tradition, as it serves as a source of stability and provides a framework for social harmony.

In contrast to classical liberalism, conservative liberals place greater emphasis on the role of government in maintaining social order, preserving moral values, and promoting social cohesion. They argue that the state should play a role in safeguarding societal institutions, including the family, religious institutions, and the rule of law, as they are seen as integral to maintaining social stability and a sense of shared identity.

Conservative liberals are often skeptical of radical or rapid social change, preferring an evolutionary rather than revolutionary approach. They argue that society should progress in a way that respects the accumulated wisdom of the past and avoids unintended consequences. They see a role for government in managing societal change and preventing disruptions that could undermine social order or erode traditional values.

Conservative liberals acknowledge that social welfare programs and safety nets have a role to play in mitigating social inequalities and providing a safety net for those in need. However, they typically advocate for market-based solutions and private initiatives over expansive state-led interventions.

To sum up, conservative liberalism combines the principles of individual freedom, limited government, and free markets with a recognition of the value of tradition, social order, and stability. It seeks to strike a balance between progress and preservation, embracing gradual societal change while preserving traditional institutions and values. Conservative liberals believe that the state should play a role in maintaining social cohesion and protecting the social fabric, while also respecting individual rights and promoting economic freedom.

Green

Green liberalism, also known as eco-liberalism, is an ideological approach that seeks to integrate environmental sustainability and ecological concerns with liberal principles. It combines elements of both liberalism and environmentalism, advocating for a market-based approach to environmental issues and the promotion of sustainable development.

Green liberals argue that environmental protection and economic growth are not mutually exclusive, but rather can be achieved through innovative market mechanisms and technological advancements. They support policies that encourage environmentally friendly practices and green technologies while also promoting economic prosperity.

At the core of green liberalism is the belief in the importance of individual liberties and free markets. Green liberals emphasize that individuals should be free to make environmentally conscious choices, and they advocate for market-driven solutions that incentivize sustainable practices. They argue that a well-regulated market can drive businesses and consumers to adopt environmentally friendly practices, such as renewable energy sources and eco-friendly products.

Green liberals also advocate for policies that internalize environmental costs, such as carbon pricing, to encourage businesses and individuals to consider the environmental impact of their activities. They believe that by factoring in the true cost of environmental damage, market forces can steer economic activities towards more sustainable practices.

Furthermore, green liberals support international cooperation to address global environmental challenges, recognizing that environmental issues transcend national borders and require collective action. They believe in the importance of global agreements and collaboration to tackle issues such as climate change and biodiversity loss effectively.

In summary, green liberalism represents an ideological fusion of liberal principles with environmental concerns. It seeks to find a balance between economic growth and environmental sustainability, advocating for market-based solutions and individual freedoms as a means to address environmental challenges. Green liberals prioritize policies that promote sustainable development, foster technological innovation, and encourage environmentally responsible choices, all while upholding the core values of liberalism.

Modern

Modern liberalism, also known as progressive liberalism, is a contemporary political ideology that builds upon the principles of classical liberalism while advocating for a more active role of government in addressing societal challenges and promoting social justice. It emphasizes the need for government intervention to protect individual rights, ensure economic opportunity, and provide essential social services.

Modern liberals believe that the government should play a significant role in addressing social and economic inequalities. They advocate for policies such as progressive taxation, social safety nets, and government-funded healthcare and education to create a more equitable society. Modern liberals also support regulations to protect consumers, workers, and the environment, as they see these measures as necessary to prevent abuses of power and ensure fair competition.

National

National liberalism is a political ideology that combines elements of both liberal and nationalist principles. It emerged in the 19th century and gained traction as a response to the changing political landscape characterized by the rise of nationalism and the demand for self-determination.

National liberals advocate for individual freedoms and civil liberties, similar to classical liberalism, but they also emphasize the importance of national identity, culture, and sovereignty. They believe that a strong nation-state is necessary to protect and promote the interests of its citizens and to preserve the unique characteristics of a nation's culture and heritage.

While national liberals support the idea of a liberal democratic system, they often prioritize the interests of their own nation above those of others. They may advocate for policies that promote domestic industries, protect national borders, and preserve national traditions. Additionally, they may be more cautious about international engagements and alliances that they perceive as potentially undermining their country's autonomy or cultural integrity.

National liberalism has evolved over time and can take on different forms in various countries. In some instances, it has been associated with more conservative positions, especially on issues related to immigration and social values. In other cases, it has aligned with progressive ideals, emphasizing inclusive national identities and supporting social and economic equality within the nation.

Like other political ideologies, national liberalism can vary significantly based on historical and cultural contexts, and its impact on policy and governance depends on the specific goals and values of the parties or movements that adopt it.

Neo

Neoliberalism is a political and economic ideology that emerged in the late 20th century, emphasizing free-market capitalism, limited government intervention, and individual freedom. Neoliberal proponents advocate for reducing state control over the economy, promoting deregulation, privatization, and free trade. They believe that market competition and the pursuit of self-interest lead to efficient resource allocation and economic growth. Neoliberal policies often prioritize reducing government spending, cutting taxes, and minimizing welfare programs. However, critics argue that neoliberalism can exacerbate economic inequality, weaken social safety nets, and prioritize profit over social welfare. The ideology's influence has been profound, shaping economic policies in many countries and influencing international organizations like the World Bank and the International Monetary Fund.

Ordo

Ordoliberalism is a German economic and political philosophy that emerged in the early 20th century and gained prominence after World War II. It is associated with the "Freiburg School" of economic thought.

At its core, ordoliberalism emphasizes the importance of a well-functioning market economy but also recognizes the necessity of state intervention to ensure fair competition and prevent market failures. Unlike laissez-faire liberalism, which advocates for minimal government intervention in the economy, ordoliberalism allows a role for the state in creating and maintaining the framework within which markets operate. This is done with the goal of allowing the greatest market freedom that can be achieved without significant drawbacks.

Key principles of ordoliberalism include the establishment of strong competition policies, clear and stable legal frameworks, and independent regulatory authorities. These measures aim to prevent monopolies, cartels, and other anti-competitive practices that could undermine market efficiency and harm consumers.

Ordoliberalism also places a strong emphasis on monetary stability and fiscal responsibility. It advocates for sound monetary policies and the avoidance of excessive government borrowing to maintain economic stability and prevent inflation.

Radical

Radical liberalism, also known as classical radicalism, emerged as the left-wing or more progressive faction within liberalism during the 18th and 19th centuries. It represents a more radical and transformative interpretation of liberal principles, advocating for broad social and political reforms to achieve greater equality, individual freedom, and social justice.

Unlike conservative or moderate liberals of the time, radical liberals sought to challenge established institutions, social hierarchies, and political structures that they perceived as impediments to individual liberty and progress. They believed that meaningful change required more than incremental reforms and instead called for sweeping transformations of society.

Radical liberals were strong proponents of universal suffrage and equal political representation, seeking to expand democratic participation beyond the narrow elites that dominated politics during that era. They also advocated for civil liberties, freedom of the press, and the abolition of oppressive laws that restricted individual rights.

Moreover, radical liberals were often vocal critics of the economic disparities prevalent in their societies. They called for economic reforms to address poverty, advocate for workers' rights, and reduce the influence of powerful economic interests over government policies.

In the 19th century, radical liberals played a crucial role in advocating for progressive causes, including the abolition of slavery, labor rights, and women's suffrage. Their ideas and activism paved the way for many of the social and political changes that followed.

Social

Social liberalism is a political ideology that combines liberal principles with a strong emphasis on social justice, equality, and the use of government intervention to address social and economic inequalities. It shares some similarities with modern liberalism but places a greater emphasis on the role of the state in promoting social welfare and ensuring a fair and just society.

At its core, social liberalism advocates for the protection of individual rights and freedoms while recognizing that these rights can only be fully realized in a society that provides equal opportunities for all its members. Social liberals argue that the state has a responsibility to address systemic inequalities and to create conditions that enable individuals to achieve their full potential.

Social liberals advocate for a mixed economy, where a combination of free market mechanisms and government intervention are used to address social issues and promote economic growth. They believe that certain services, such as healthcare, education, and social security, should be provided or heavily regulated by the government to ensure that they are accessible to all members of society, regardless of their economic status.

Moreover, social liberals champion progressive taxation as a means of funding social programs and redistributing wealth from the affluent to the less fortunate. They argue that a progressive tax system can help reduce income inequality and provide resources for essential public services and social safety nets.

In terms of social issues, social liberals are often at the forefront of advocating for civil rights.They believe that the government should play a role in protecting the rights and dignity of marginalized and vulnerable groups, and in dismantling discriminatory laws and practices.

Social liberalism also recognizes the importance of environmental sustainability and the need to address climate change. Social liberals often support policies and regulations aimed at protecting the environment and promoting sustainable development.

While social liberalism emphasizes the role of the state in promoting social justice and equality, it also seeks to strike a balance between government intervention and individual freedom. Social liberals recognize that excessive state control can be detrimental to personal liberties and economic innovation, and they aim to find a middle ground that fosters both individual freedom and social progress.

In conclusion, social liberalism is a political ideology that combines liberal principles with a commitment to social justice, equality, and government intervention. It emphasizes the role of the state in addressing social and economic inequalities, providing social welfare, and promoting the well-being of all members of society. Social liberals seek to create a fair and just society that ensures individual rights, equal opportunities, and environmental sustainability.

Techno

Technoliberalism is a political ideology that embraces technological innovation and its potential to drive societal progress and individual empowerment. It advocates for the use of technology, particularly digital technologies and the internet, to foster economic growth, enhance personal freedom, and promote global interconnectedness. Technoliberals often believe that market forces and entrepreneurship, facilitated by technological advancements, can solve various social and economic challenges. However, they also emphasize the importance of responsible regulation to ensure consumer protection, privacy rights, and fair competition. Technoliberalism aims to strike a balance between promoting technological development and safeguarding the public interest, envisioning a future where technology serves as a force for positive change and human flourishing.

Libertarianism

Libertarianism is a political ideology that emphasizes individual liberty, limited government, and free-market capitalism. Rooted in the principles of classical liberalism, libertarianism advocates for minimal state intervention in both the economic and social spheres, promoting personal freedom and autonomy as its core values.

At the heart of libertarianism is the belief that individuals have inherent rights to life, liberty, and property, and that the role of government should be restricted to protecting these rights and maintaining the rule of law. Libertarians argue that government intervention often leads to unintended consequences, inefficiencies, and the infringement of individual freedoms.

Economically, libertarians advocate for free-market capitalism, where the forces of supply and demand determine prices, and private property rights are respected. They argue that a competitive market allows for the most efficient allocation of resources and provides opportunities for innovation and prosperity.

In terms of social issues, libertarians generally support personal autonomy and oppose laws that limit individual choices, whether they pertain to personal relationships, lifestyle choices, or consensual activities.

There are various branches of libertarianism, ranging from minarchism, which advocates for a limited government solely responsible for protecting individual rights and enforcing contracts, to anarcho-capitalism, which calls for the abolition of government altogether, relying instead on voluntary associations and private institutions to address societal needs.

Critics of libertarianism argue that its emphasis on minimal government intervention may lead to the neglect of essential public goods and services, such as education, healthcare, and environmental protection. They contend that unchecked capitalism can lead to wealth inequality and the exploitation of workers.

Despite these criticisms, libertarianism has influenced political discourse and policy-making in many countries. It has found support among various individuals and groups, from free-market economists and small-government advocates to civil liberties activists.

Libertarian ideas have been incorporated into political parties and movements worldwide, although achieving significant electoral success remains a challenge due to the broad diversity of libertarian perspectives and the nuanced nature of their policy proposals.

Longism

Huey Long, also known as "The Kingfish," was a prominent American politician who advocated for a populist and redistributive ideology known as Longism. As the Governor of Louisiana from 1928 to 1932 and later a U.S. Senator, Long championed policies aimed at alleviating poverty, providing economic opportunities, and challenging the concentration of wealth and power.

Longism sought to address the inequalities and economic hardships faced by the working class and rural poor during the Great Depression. Long proposed a series of reforms, including wealth redistribution, progressive taxation, public works programs, and increased access to education and healthcare. He believed that the government had a responsibility to provide for the well-being of its citizens and that a fairer distribution of wealth was necessary to achieve social and economic justice.

While Long's ideology drew inspiration from populism and New Deal policies, his methods were often controversial. He centralized power in Louisiana, leading to accusations of political corruption and authoritarian tendencies. Nevertheless, his charismatic leadership and ability to connect with ordinary Americans made him a popular figure, especially among those struggling with economic hardship.

Long's influence and potential for broader national impact were cut short when he was assassinated in 1935. However, his ideas continued to resonate, inspiring later politicians and social movements that sought to address income inequality and advocate for progressive policies.

Marxism

Introduction

Marxism, developed by Karl Marx and Friedrich Engels in the 19th century, is a comprehensive political ideology that has left an indelible mark on the global socio-political landscape. Rooted in the analysis of class struggle and the critique of capitalism, Marxism has shaped numerous political movements, revolutions, and theories throughout history. This article explores the core tenets and key principles of Marxism, highlighting its impact and relevance in contemporary society.

Class Struggle and Historical Materialism

At the heart of Marxism lies the concept of class struggle, which asserts that society is fundamentally divided into antagonistic social classes that are in conflict with one another. According to Marxism, history is shaped by these class struggles, where the dominant class in any given epoch exploits and oppresses the subordinate class. This theory, known as historical materialism, views the mode of production as the primary driver of social change and class dynamics.

Critique of Capitalism

Marxism offers a comprehensive critique of capitalism, arguing that it is an inherently exploitative system that perpetuates inequality and alienation. Capitalism, in Marxist theory, is characterized by the private ownership of the means of production, where the bourgeoisie (the capitalist class) exploits the proletariat (the working class) for surplus value. Marxists argue that capitalism inherently prioritizes profit accumulation over the well-being of the workers, leading to economic disparities and social alienation.

Economic Determinism and Socialism

Marxism posits that the contradictions within capitalism will inevitably lead to its own downfall, as the exploited proletariat becomes conscious of its exploitation and organizes for social change. This process, known as economic determinism, ultimately paves the way for the establishment of socialism. Socialism, as envisioned by Marxism, entails the collective ownership of the means of production and the establishment of a classless society, where the principle of "from each according to their ability, to each according to their needs" is realized.

Role of the Proletariat and Revolution

Marxism places great importance on the role of the proletariat in revolutionary change. The working class, according to Marxists, possesses the potential to overthrow capitalism through a proletarian revolution. This revolution aims to seize control of the means of production from the bourgeoisie and establish a socialist society. Marxists argue that the organized working class, through their collective action, has the power to transform society and create a more equitable and just order.

Criticism and Adaptations

While Marxism has had a profound impact on political thought and practice, it has also faced substantial criticism. Critics argue that Marxist theories neglect individual agency, overestimate the inevitability of revolution, and downplay the complexities of human nature and cultural diversity. Moreover, the historical implementation of Marxism in various countries has raised concerns about authoritarianism and the concentration of power.

In response to these criticisms, contemporary Marxist thinkers have developed diverse adaptations and variations of the ideology. These include democratic socialism, which combines Marxist principles with democratic institutions, and analytical Marxism, which seeks to integrate Marxist ideas with modern social sciences. These adaptations aim to address some of the shortcomings of classical Marxism and make it more applicable to the complexities of the modern world.

Analytical

Analytical Marxism, also known as rational choice Marxism or scientific Marxism, is a sub-ideology of Marxism that emerged in the late 20th century. It sought to apply rigorous analytical and empirical methods, often drawn from economics and social sciences, to understand and advance Marxist theory.

One of the key objectives of analytical Marxism was to clarify and refine Marxist concepts while making them compatible with modern social science methodologies. Advocates of analytical Marxism aimed to address some of the perceived weaknesses in traditional Marxist thought, such as the lack of precision in concepts like exploitation and class struggle.

Analytical Marxists focused on developing precise definitions of key Marxist terms and constructing formal models to analyze capitalist societies and the dynamics of class struggle. They also sought to integrate Marxist ideas with other social theories, like rational choice theory and game theory, to deepen their understanding of complex social phenomena.

Furthermore, analytical Marxism aimed to avoid dogmatism and open Marxist theory to critical scrutiny. Instead of treating Marxist texts as sacred texts, analytical Marxists encouraged a critical engagement with Marx's writings and emphasized the importance of empirical evidence and logical consistency in developing Marxist theories.

Prominent figures associated with analytical Marxism include Jon Elster, G.A. Cohen, and Erik Olin Wright, among others. Their work has significantly enriched Marxist scholarship and fostered interdisciplinary dialogue between Marxism and the social sciences.

While analytical Marxism has influenced Marxist scholarship and introduced valuable methodological tools, it remains one among many diverse approaches within the broader Marxist tradition. Some critics argue that it risks becoming overly abstract and detached from real-world political struggles, while others appreciate its effort to engage with modern social science methods in advancing Marxist analysis.

Austro

Austro-Marxism was a distinctive strand of Marxist thought that emerged in Austria during the late 19th and early 20th centuries. It sought to adapt and revise traditional Marxist theory to address the specific socio-economic conditions of the Austro-Hungarian Empire. Key figures associated with Austro-Marxism included Karl Renner, Otto Bauer, and Max Adler. Unlike orthodox Marxism, Austro-Marxists emphasized the importance of national and cultural identities, recognizing the diverse nationalities within the multi-ethnic empire. They advocated for a democratic and decentralized socialist state that would accommodate the autonomy of different national groups. Austro-Marxism also focused on the role of intellectuals and their influence in shaping societal change. Despite its intellectual contributions, Austro-Marxism faced challenges due to the collapse of the Austro-Hungarian Empire after World War I and the rise of authoritarianism in the interwar period. Nevertheless, its ideas continued to influence socialist thought and contributed to debates within the broader Marxist tradition.

Leninism

See *Marxism-Leninism*.

Luxemburgism

Rosa Luxemburg was a prominent Marxist theorist and revolutionary socialist who made significant contributions to the socialist movement in the early 20th century. Her ideology, often referred to as Luxemburgism, was a blend of Marxism and revolutionary internationalism.

One of the central elements of Luxemburg's ideology was her emphasis on the importance of mass action and the spontaneity of working-class movements. She believed that revolutionary change could not be orchestrated solely by a vanguard party but required the active participation and self-organization of the working class.

Luxemburg also critiqued the reformist tendencies within the socialist movement, arguing that gradual reforms within the capitalist system were insufficient to achieve socialism. She advocated for a revolutionary break with the capitalist order through the establishment of a democratically governed workers' state.

Furthermore, Luxemburg was a staunch opponent of imperialism and militarism, denouncing World War I as an imperialist conflict. Her anti-war activism led to her imprisonment during the war.

In her seminal work, "The Accumulation of Capital," Luxemburg also offered an influential analysis of what Marxism views as capitalism's inherent contradictions, particularly focusing on the need for continuous expansion into non-capitalist markets. This work remains significant in debates surrounding the dynamics of capitalism and imperialism.

Rosa Luxemburg's legacy continues to inspire left-wing movements and thinkers today. Her unwavering commitment to mass action, international solidarity, and revolutionary change has made her an enduring figure in the history of socialist thought and activism.

Maoism

Maoism, also known as Mao Zedong Thought, is a political ideology and form of Marxism-Leninism that emerged as a significant school of thought within the communist movement, primarily in China. It is named after Mao Zedong, the leader of the Chinese Communist Party and the founding father of the People's Republic of China.

Maoism places a strong emphasis on the role of the peasantry as a revolutionary force and the importance of mobilizing the rural population in the struggle against feudalism, imperialism, and capitalism. Mao argued that in countries with large agrarian populations like China, the peasantry, rather than the urban working class, could serve as the vanguard of the revolution.

Central to Maoism is the concept of "protracted people's war," a strategy that involves a prolonged, guerrilla-style armed struggle by the masses, culminating in a final phase of conventional warfare to seize power. This strategy was successfully employed in the Chinese Communist Party's victory over the Nationalist forces during the Chinese Civil War.

Mao also promoted the idea of "mass line," which stressed the need for communist leaders to maintain close ties with the ordinary people and take their needs and aspirations into account. The mass line aimed to prevent bureaucratization and ensure that policies were rooted in the concerns of the masses.

Maoism also emphasized the importance of "continuous revolution" and the need for ongoing class struggle even after the communist party had assumed power. This idea led to the establishment of mass campaigns, such as the Great Leap Forward and the Cultural Revolution, which sought to mobilize the masses to challenge and reshape society continually.

After Mao's death in 1976, Maoism underwent various interpretations and diverged into different schools of thought. Today, while it continues to influence some revolutionary movements and communist parties, it is not as widespread as other branches of Marxism. Nevertheless, Mao Zedong and Maoist principles remain significant in Chinese politics, with his portrait still featured on the Tiananmen Gate in Beijing as a symbol of the Chinese Communist Party's legacy.

Post Marxism

Post-Marxism is an intellectual and theoretical development that emerged in the late 20th century as a critical reevaluation and revision of classical Marxism. It represents a departure from orthodox Marxist thought while retaining its core concerns with power, class struggle, and social transformation.

One of the key aspects of post-Marxism is its rejection of economic determinism, a central tenet of classical Marxism, which posits that economic factors determine the trajectory of history and societal change. Post-Marxists argue for a broader understanding of power dynamics, acknowledging the significance of cultural, discursive, and ideological factors in shaping social relations and inequality.

Influenced by poststructuralist and postmodernist thought, post-Marxists emphasize the role of language, representation, and identity in the construction of meaning and power relations. They explore how discourse and cultural practices shape subjectivity, challenging fixed notions of class and identity.

Ernesto Laclau and Chantal Mouffe are two prominent theorists associated with post-Marxism. They developed the theory of "radical democracy," which advocates for pluralism, agonism, and the acknowledgment of multiple social conflicts. Instead of seeking to establish a unified working-class movement as the sole agent of change, post-Marxists argue for building alliances and coalitions among diverse social groups, including feminist, environmental, and anti-racist movements.

Post-Marxism also engages with postcolonial theory and intersectionality, recognizing the complexities of oppression and highlighting the interconnectedness of various struggles for emancipation. By broadening the scope of analysis beyond class-based exploitation, post-Marxism aims to address multiple axes of domination and subordination.

Critics of post-Marxism argue that its emphasis on discourse and cultural factors downplays the importance of material conditions and economic relations in understanding social inequality. Some also contend that the rejection of universal claims and the focus on diversity can lead to a fragmentation of progressive politics.

Despite these criticisms, post-Marxism has significantly influenced contemporary debates on political theory, cultural studies, and social movements. Its efforts to update Marxist thought for the complexities of the modern world continue to shape progressive scholarship and activism, contributing to ongoing discussions about the nature of power, identity, and social change in the 21st century.

Revisionist Marxism

Revisionist Marxism, also known as reformist Marxism or evolutionary socialism, is a strand of thought that seeks to update and modify classical Marxist theory to adapt to changing social and economic conditions. Revisionists often critique some of the original tenets of Marxism while still acknowledging its core concerns with class struggle and inequality.

One of the main points of departure for revisionist Marxists is their rejection of the inevitability of revolution as the primary means of achieving socialist goals. Instead, they advocate for incremental reforms within the existing capitalist system, believing that a gradual transformation can lead to a more just and equitable society. This approach often involves working within democratic institutions to achieve social and economic changes through the political process.

Revisionist Marxists also emphasize the role of the state as a potential agent for progressive change. They believe that the state can play a positive role in regulating the economy, providing social services, and mitigating the worst excesses of capitalism.

Eduard Bernstein, a prominent figure within the Social Democratic Party of Germany in the late 19th and early 20th centuries, is often considered one of the key proponents of revisionist Marxism. He argued that Marx's predictions of inevitable economic crises and the collapse of capitalism were not borne out by empirical evidence, leading him to advocate for a more pragmatic and reform-oriented approach to socialism.

Despite criticism from orthodox Marxists who see revisionism as a dilution of revolutionary principles, revisionist Marxism has had a significant impact on social democratic movements in various countries. Many modern social democratic parties embrace revisionist ideas, promoting a mixed economy, social welfare programs, and a focus on democratic governance while still working towards more egalitarian and just societies.

Trotskyism

Trotskyism is a political ideology and a form of Marxism that is based on the ideas and theories of Leon Trotsky, a prominent revolutionary and one of the leading figures of the Russian Revolution. Trotskyism emerged as a distinct ideological current within the broader Marxist movement, and it continues to influence leftist politics worldwide.

One of the key elements of Trotskyism is its emphasis on permanent revolution. Trotsky argued that in countries where capitalism was not fully developed, the working class could lead a socialist revolution and establish a workers' state. However, he also believed that in such countries, the revolution would need to spread internationally to succeed and avoid being isolated and crushed by capitalist powers.

Trotskyism also rejected the concept of socialism in one country, which was promoted by Joseph Stalin and the Soviet leadership. Trotskyists viewed the establishment of socialism within the confines of a single country as leading to bureaucratic degeneration and a distortion of Marxist principles.

Furthermore, Trotskyism upheld the principles of workers' democracy and called for the active participation of workers in decision-making processes, both within the party and in the construction of a socialist society.

After Trotsky's exile and assassination, Trotskyism fragmented into various tendencies and organizations, each with its interpretations of his ideas and strategies for achieving socialist goals. Trotskyist movements have often been active participants in workers' struggles, anti-war movements, and social justice campaigns across the world.

Despite being a minority current within the broader left-wing spectrum, Trotskyism remains influential and continues to inspire political activists and intellectuals committed to revolutionary change and the establishment of a classless and egalitarian society.

Western Marxism

Western Marxism refers to a diverse set of Marxist theories and interpretations that emerged in the Western world during the 20th century. Unlike the Soviet-dominated orthodox Marxism, Western Marxists focused on cultural, philosophical, and sociological dimensions of Marxism, rather than adhering strictly to economic determinism.

Prominent thinkers within Western Marxism include Antonio Gramsci, who emphasized the importance of cultural hegemony and the role of intellectuals in shaping societal norms and values. Gramsci argued that achieving socialist transformation required a "war of position" to challenge dominant ideologies and institutions.

Another influential figure was Georg Lukács, who explored the concept of reification and the alienation of labor under capitalism. Lukács also delved into the significance of class consciousness in revolutionary praxis.

The Frankfurt School, particularly Theodor Adorno, Max Horkheimer, and Herbert Marcuse, also played a central role in Western Marxism. Their critical theory focused on the role of culture, mass media, and ideology in perpetuating social inequality. Founded in the 1920s, the Frankfurt School's primary focus was examining the role of culture, media, and ideology in perpetuating social inequality and oppression.The Frankfurt School's work aimed to understand and critique the capitalist system and the rise of authoritarianism, emphasizing the importance of culture and the media in shaping public consciousness. They sought to bring about social change through philosophical reflection, cultural critique, and challenging the prevailing capitalist order.

Western Marxists often engaged in interdisciplinary studies, drawing insights from sociology, psychology, and literary theory. They critiqued the bureaucratic tendencies of orthodox Marxism and explored new avenues for Marxist thought, promoting a more humanistic and democratic interpretation of Marxism.

In summary, Western Marxism represents a diverse and intellectually rich tradition of Marxist thought in the Western world. Its emphasis on cultural and social aspects, as well as its interdisciplinary approach, has left a lasting impact on the study of Marxism and broader social theory.

Marxism-Leninism

Introduction

Marxism-Leninism is an ideology that emerged as a significant development within the Marxist tradition. It was primarily shaped by the thoughts and actions of Vladimir Lenin, who adapted and expanded upon the ideas of Karl Marx and Friedrich Engels. While orthodox Marxists may have reservations or concerns about certain aspects of Marxism-Leninism, it is crucial to explore its principles, historical context, and contributions to the socialist movement.

Origins and Historical Context

Marxism-Leninism arose in the early 20th century as a response to the socio-political conditions prevalent in Russia at the time. Lenin believed that the development of capitalism had created a revolutionary potential among the proletariat, but he also recognized the need for a vanguard party to guide the revolution and establish a proletarian state. This adaptation of Marxist theory to the specific conditions of Russia is one of the defining characteristics of Marxism-Leninism.

The Role of the Vanguard Party

One of the central tenets of Marxism-Leninism is the necessity of a vanguard party composed of politically conscious and dedicated revolutionaries. The vanguard party is seen as the driving force behind the revolution, organizing the working class, and leading the struggle against capitalism and imperialism. Orthodox Marxists might question the hierarchical structure of the vanguard party, but Lenin argued that it was a temporary stage on the path to communism, necessary to overcome the resistance of the ruling class.

Imperialism and Anti-Colonial Struggles

Marxism-Leninism also places significant emphasis on the global struggle against imperialism and colonialism. Lenin argued that imperialism was the highest stage of capitalism, marked by the monopolistic control of resources, markets, and territories by powerful nations. Orthodox Marxists might agree with the critique of imperialism but may have differing perspectives on the strategies employed to combat it. Marxism-Leninism sought to forge alliances with anti-colonial movements, recognizing their potential to weaken imperialism and create conditions for socialist revolution.

Dictatorship of the Proletariat

Lenin's interpretation of the dictatorship of the proletariat is another key aspect of Marxism-Leninism. Orthodox Marxists may have reservations about the term "dictatorship" as it implies authoritarianism, but Lenin argued that it was necessary to suppress the counterrevolutionary forces and consolidate the gains of the revolution. He envisioned the dictatorship of the proletariat as a state in which the working class held political power, paving the way for the eventual withering away of the state and the establishment of a classless society.

Socialist Construction and Planned Economy

Marxism-Leninism places a strong emphasis on the construction of socialism and the transition from capitalism to communism. Lenin argued that the proletariat must seize control of the means of production and establish a planned economy, where resources are allocated based on social needs rather than profit. This approach aimed to overcome the contradictions of capitalism and lay the foundation for a classless society. However, orthodox Marxists may debate the extent of centralization and the potential for bureaucratization under such a system.

Conclusion
Marxism-Leninism represents a distinct branch within the Marxist tradition that evolved in response to the specific historical and political context of Russia. From the vanguard party and anti-imperialism to the dictatorship of the proletariat and planned economy, Marxism-Leninism sought to adapt Marxist theory to the conditions of the time. Engaging in critical dialogue and analysis of different Marxist perspectives allows for a deeper understanding of the complexities and diversities within the socialist tradition.

Metaxism

Metaxism is a political ideology that emerged in Greece during the 1930s under the leadership of Ioannis Metaxas. It sought to establish a corporatist and authoritarian state, combining elements of nationalism, fascism, and traditionalism.

Metaxism aimed to create a unified and disciplined society by emphasizing the importance of social harmony and collective identity. It rejected liberal democracy and promoted a hierarchical social structure, with the state as the supreme authority. Metaxas sought to strengthen the role of the state in all aspects of life, including the economy, education, and culture.

The ideology emphasized the primacy of the nation, celebrating Greek culture and heritage. Metaxism aimed to revive the spirit of ancient Greece and restore Greece's past glory. It promoted the concept of the "Third Hellenic Civilization," emphasizing the unique contribution of Greek culture to world history.

Metaxism implemented policies to promote economic self-sufficiency, protect local industries, and enhance national unity. It sought to suppress political opposition and dissent through strict censorship and the suppression of civil liberties.

Nationalism

Nationalism is a complex and multifaceted ideology that centers around a deep sense of collective identity and loyalty to a specific nation or group of people. It emphasizes the importance of shared history, culture, language, and territory as defining characteristics of the nation. Nationalists believe in the uniqueness and superiority of their nation and seek to preserve and promote its interests, values, and traditions.

At its core, nationalism seeks to foster a strong sense of unity and solidarity among members of a nation, often leading to a sense of pride and patriotism. It can serve as a powerful force for mobilizing people towards common goals such as achieving independence, preserving cultural heritage, or defending national sovereignty.

Nationalism can manifest in various forms, ranging from civic nationalism, which emphasizes shared values and citizenship, to ethnic nationalism, which is based on common ancestry and ethnicity. Cultural and religious nationalism also exist, where the focus is on preserving and promoting a specific cultural or religious identity within the nation.

Throughout history, nationalism has played a significant role in shaping political movements, revolutions, and the formation of nation-states. It has influenced decolonization movements, struggles for independence, and the redrawing of borders after wars. In the modern era, nationalism continues to be a prominent force in shaping political discourse and policies in many countries.

New Left

The New Left was a political and social movement that emerged in the 1960s and 1970s as a response to the perceived failures and shortcomings of the traditional left and the prevailing political establishment. Unlike the old left, which was often associated with Marxist-Leninist ideologies and hierarchical party structures, the New Left sought to distance itself from traditional communist and socialist organizations.

The New Left was a diverse and loosely connected movement that included student activists, civil rights advocates, anti-war protesters, feminists, environmentalists, and others. It was characterized by a more decentralized and participatory approach to decision-making, rejecting the top-down organizational style of the traditional left. Grassroots organizing, direct action, and political mobilization were central to the New Left's strategy for effecting social change.

The movement was highly critical of the political establishment, corporate power, and the military-industrial complex. It opposed the Vietnam War and advocated for peace and disarmament. It also campaigned for civil rights, gender equality, and environmental protection. The New Left challenged traditional norms and values, questioning authority and advocating for greater personal freedom and individual expression.

One of the prominent ideas that emerged from the New Left was the concept of participatory democracy, which emphasized the direct involvement of citizens in decision-making processes. This notion rejected the idea of representative democracy as insufficient in addressing social issues and sought to give individuals a more active role in shaping their communities and society.

The New Left also embraced a more inclusive approach to social justice, seeking to bridge the gap between different social movements and promote solidarity among diverse groups.

While the New Left as a distinct movement waned in the 1970s, its impact was profound and enduring. Many of its ideals and strategies have been integrated into contemporary progressive movements, continuing to shape political activism worldwide.

Radical Centrism

In today's highly polarized political landscape, the concept of radical centrism has emerged as an alternative approach that seeks to bridge ideological divides and promote effective governance. Rooted in the principles of pragmatism and balance, radical centrism advocates for a nuanced and inclusive approach to policymaking.

Defining Radical Centrism:

Radical centrism, also known as the radical middle or new center, represents a political ideology that rejects the traditional left-right spectrum in favor of a more nuanced and pragmatic perspective. It emphasizes the pursuit of practical solutions that draw from a range of political ideologies while avoiding extreme positions. Radical centrists strive to transcend partisan divisions and embrace a holistic approach that considers diverse perspectives.

Key Tenets of Radical Centrism:

- Pragmatism: Radical centrism places a strong emphasis on practicality and problem-solving. Instead of adhering rigidly to ideological dogma, centrists seek evidence-based policies that address real-world challenges. This pragmatic approach allows for flexibility and adaptability in policymaking, enabling politicians to respond to changing circumstances effectively.

- Balance: Radical centrism promotes the idea of finding a middle ground between competing interests. It acknowledges the value of compromise and consensus-building, seeking to bridge divides and foster collaboration among diverse groups. By considering multiple viewpoints, centrists aim to develop solutions that reflect the broad interests of society.

- Evidence and Reason: Central to radical centrism is a commitment to rationality and evidence-based decision-making. Centrists value scientific research, expert analysis, and data-driven approaches to policy formulation. By relying on empirical evidence rather than ideological biases, centrists aim to craft policies that are effective and beneficial for all.

Reactionary

Reactionary political ideology is characterized by a strong desire to return to or preserve past social, political, and cultural norms. Reactionaries oppose progressive or liberal ideas and advocate for a return to traditional values, institutions, and hierarchical structures. They believe that the changes brought about by modernity, social movements, and liberalization have led to the erosion of societal order and moral values.

Reactionaries often view the past with nostalgia, perceiving it as a time of stability and order that should be reinstated. They may reject democratic principles, favoring a return to authoritarian rule or monarchical systems. In some cases, religion plays a significant role in shaping their beliefs, and they seek to uphold the dominance of a particular faith in public and private life.

Unlike conservatives who aim to preserve existing institutions while acknowledging the need for incremental changes, reactionaries seek a more radical and comprehensive reversal of societal transformations.

Historically, reactionary movements have emerged in response to revolutionary or liberal movements, seeking to roll back the gains made by progressive forces. While reactionaries often assert that their ideology will restore stability and moral values, critics argue that their vision risks stifling progress, diversity, and human rights.

As with any political ideology, the manifestations and degrees of reactionism can vary significantly across different societies and historical contexts. However, the common thread among reactionaries is a fervent opposition to change and a longing for a return to a perceived golden age.

Reactionary Modernism

Reactionary modernism is a complex ideological current that emerged in the early 20th century. It represents a fusion of traditionalism and a desire for modernity, often seeking to revive or reinvent elements of the past in response to perceived threats posed by modernization and social change. Proponents of reactionary modernism reject liberal democracy and Enlightenment values, advocating instead for strong centralized authority and authoritarianism.

In some cases, reactionary modernists idealized technological progress, industrialization, and the rationalization of society, while simultaneously embracing reactionary and traditional social ideologies. They sought to reconcile modernity's advancements with nostalgic visions of a glorified past. One notable example of reactionary modernism was found in the early years of Nazi Germany, where elements of modern industrial and technological achievements were harnessed to serve the goals of an oppressive and racially exclusive regime.

Salazarism

The ideology of Salazar and the Estado Novo in Portugal was a conservative and authoritarian political system that lasted from 1933 to 1974. António de Oliveira Salazar, a conservative economist and statesman, became the Prime Minister of Portugal in 1932 and established the Estado Novo ("New State") to bring stability and control to a country facing economic challenges and political unrest.

Salazar's ideology was rooted in traditional Catholic values, corporatism, and anti-communism. He sought to maintain strong ties with the Catholic Church and emphasized the importance of family, religion, and hierarchy in society. The Estado Novo aimed to establish a centralized and authoritarian regime, with Salazar holding significant power and control over the government and institutions.

The regime relied on censorship, secret police, and suppression of political opposition to maintain authority. The ideology promoted a "spirit of unity" and discouraged political pluralism or dissenting views. The Estado Novo also upheld a paternalistic approach, where the state assumed a role as the protector and guardian of the nation, guiding its citizens towards the common good.

Economically, Salazar's regime favored corporatism, which involved cooperation between the state, labor unions, and business interests. It aimed to balance the interests of different social classes while maintaining control over the economy. Salazar implemented policies of autarky, seeking self-sufficiency and economic independence from other countries.

While the Estado Novo initially brought stability and economic growth to Portugal, over time, it faced mounting criticism for its perceived oppressive practices and lack of political freedoms. In 1974, the Carnation Revolution led to the overthrow of the dictatorship and the establishment of a democratic government in Portugal, bringing an end to Salazar's ideology and the Estado Novo era.

Showa Statism

Showa Statism refers to the political and ideological system that characterized Japan during the reign of Emperor Hirohito (1926-1989), which is commonly referred to as the Shōwa era. It emerged in the 1930s and was prevalent during Japan's imperialistic expansion and throughout World War II.

Showa Statism combined elements of nationalism, militarism, and authoritarianism, aiming to strengthen the authority of the emperor and centralize power under a government led by military officials. It sought to create a unified and disciplined society based on the idea of a "spiritual mobilization" where all aspects of life, including the economy, culture, and education, were to be harnessed for the benefit of the state and its imperial ambitions.

The ideology glorified the concept of the emperor as a divine figure, imbued with a sense of sacred duty to guide and lead the nation. It promoted a sense of national unity and collective identity, often at the expense of individual freedoms and dissenting opinions.

Showa Statism was characterized by the dominance of the military in the government and decision-making processes. The military exercised significant influence over policies, both domestically and in foreign affairs, and played a pivotal role in Japan's expansionist ambitions in East Asia.

However, the militaristic policies and aggressive actions pursued under Showa Statism eventually led Japan into war with several countries, including the United States. The devastating consequences of World War II, particularly the atomic bombings of Hiroshima and Nagasaki, shattered the foundations of Showa Statism and marked the beginning of Japan's transition to a constitutional monarchy and democratic state.

Today, Showa Statism is viewed with scrutiny in Japan and abroad, as it represents a period of Japanese history characterized by militarism and expansionism.

Social Darwinism

Social Darwinism is a social and political ideology that emerged in the late 19th and early 20th centuries, drawing upon the ideas of Charles Darwin's theory of natural selection and applying them to human society. The core premise of Social Darwinism is that competition and struggle for survival among individuals and social groups lead to the advancement of societies. According to this ideology, those who are deemed to be more fit or superior in terms of intelligence, wealth, or power, are naturally destined to thrive and dominate, while the weaker or less successful individuals and groups are seen as destined to fail and fade away.

Advocates of Social Darwinism often used this ideology to justify various social and economic inequalities, arguing that such disparities were simply the result of natural and inevitable processes. They claimed that attempting to intervene or support the less fortunate would disrupt the natural order and hinder progress.

Social Darwinism has been criticized for its deterministic and reductionist approach to human society, as well as for its lack of empathy and disregard for social responsibility. Critics argued that it oversimplifies complex social issues and provides a flawed justification for discrimination and exploitation.

Social Democracy

Social democracy, a political ideology that emerged in the late 19th century, aims to reconcile the principles of democracy and socialism. Rooted in the belief that societies should prioritize social justice, economic equality, and the well-being of all citizens, social democracy has had a profound impact on numerous countries around the world.

Foundations and Core Principles:
Social democracy finds its roots in the broader socialist movement and seeks to achieve social justice through democratic means. It emphasizes the importance of a strong welfare state, economic regulation, and labor rights to address systemic inequalities. Key principles that underpin social democracy include:

- Economic Justice: Social democracy advocates for a fair distribution of wealth and resources. It aims to reduce income disparities by implementing progressive taxation systems, ensuring a living wage, and promoting social safety nets such as healthcare, education, and social security. By providing equal opportunities and protecting vulnerable groups, social democracy strives to create a more equitable society.

- Democracy and Participation: Social democracy upholds the principles of democracy, including citizen participation, human rights, and the rule of law. It emphasizes the importance of robust democratic institutions, political accountability, and protection of civil liberties. Social democrats believe that political power should be accessible to all, fostering inclusive decision-making processes and empowering marginalized communities.

- Solidarity and Social Cohesion: Social democracy values social cohesion and collective action. It promotes a sense of solidarity among citizens, recognizing that individual well-being is interconnected with the welfare of society as a whole. Through collective bargaining, labor rights, and social dialogue, social democracy aims to build strong and inclusive communities that support each other.

Legacy:

- Welfare State: Social democracy played a pivotal role in the establishment and expansion of comprehensive welfare states. These systems provide universal access to healthcare, education, housing, and social security, ensuring a basic standard of living for all citizens. Welfare states have contributed to reducing poverty, improving social mobility, and enhancing societal well-being.
- Labor Rights and Social Dialogue: Social democrats have advocated workers' rights, increased wages, safer working conditions, and the right to collective bargaining. Through strong labor movements and social dialogue, social democracy has helped establish regulations that protect workers and foster more equitable employer-employee relationships.
- Economic Regulation and Market Reforms: Social democracy recognizes the importance of a mixed economy where both public and private sectors play a role. It advocates for robust economic regulations to prevent market failures, ensure fair competition, and protect consumers. Social democrats have introduced measures such as progressive taxation, corporate accountability, and financial regulations in an attempt to promote economic stability and reduce inequality.
- Social Justice: Some social democrats been instrumental in advancing gender equality and social justice. It has championed policies such as paid parental leave, gender quotas, and anti-discrimination legislation to address gender disparities and promote equal opportunities.

Socialism

Socialism is a political ideology that aims to create what it views as more equitable and just society by advocating for the collective ownership and democratic control of the means of production. Rooted in concerns about social and economic inequality, socialism seeks to address issues of exploitation, class struggle, and the concentration of wealth and power. It encompasses a range of beliefs and approaches.

At its core, socialism challenges the structure of capitalism and advocates for a more egalitarian society. It contends that the capitalist system, driven by profit and private ownership, perpetuates inequality and social divisions. Instead, socialism promotes the idea that resources and wealth should be distributed more fairly and that decision-making power should be democratized.

One prominent strand of socialist ideology is democratic socialism. Democratic socialists believe in combining the principles of socialism with democratic governance. They advocate for a mixed economy where the means of production are collectively owned or regulated, while still allowing for individual entrepreneurship and private enterprise. Democratic socialists argue that a strong welfare state, with universal healthcare, education, and social security, is essential to ensure a fair and just society. They believe that through democratic processes, including elections and participatory decision-making, society can collectively determine its economic priorities and social policies.

Another variation of socialism is market socialism, which proposes a system where the means of production are owned and controlled by the workers themselves. Market socialists argue that economic planning and coordination can occur within a decentralized market system, ensuring efficiency and innovation while preventing exploitation. In this model, cooperatives and worker-owned enterprises play a central role, allowing workers to have a direct stake in the decision-making and the distribution of profits.

Revolutionary socialism, on the other hand, emphasizes the need for a radical transformation of society through revolutionary means. Proponents of revolutionary socialism argue that significant systemic change can only be achieved by overthrowing the capitalist system and establishing a socialist society through popular uprising. This ideology is often associated with the writings of Karl Marx and Friedrich Engels, who envisioned a classless society where the proletariat (the working class) collectively owns and controls the means of production.

Socialism has historically been a powerful force in various social and political movements. It has been a driving ideology behind labor movements, the fight for workers' rights, and struggles for social change. Socialist movements have sought to to transform various systems of power, advocating for greater economic equality and social solidarity.

Conservative

Conservative socialism, also known as right-wing socialism or social conservatism, is a unique ideological blend that combines elements of traditional socialism with conservative values and principles. Unlike traditional socialism, conservative socialism advocates for maintaining social hierarchies and traditional institutions, such as the family and religion, alongside a strong welfare state. It seeks to address social and economic inequalities through government intervention and social programs while upholding traditional values and cultural norms. Distinguishing characteristics of conservative socialism include a belief in gradual reform rather than radical revolution, an emphasis on preserving cultural and national identity, and a commitment to maintaining social order and stability. This ideological fusion seeks to strike a balance between social justice and conservative values, making it distinct from both traditional socialism and traditional conservatism.

Libertarian

Libertarian socialism, also known as anarcho-socialism or left-libertarianism, is a political ideology that seeks to combine the principles of socialism with the advocacy of individual freedom and autonomy. It envisions a society where the means of production and resources are collectively owned and managed by the community, ensuring equitable distribution of wealth and eliminating oppressive hierarchies. However, unlike traditional authoritarian forms of socialism, libertarian socialists reject the concentration of power in a centralized state and instead advocate for decentralized, self-governing communities and voluntary associations. They emphasize direct democracy, grassroots organizing, and non-hierarchical decision-making processes to empower individuals and communities. Libertarian socialism seeks to establish a society based on cooperation, mutual aid, and freedom from both state and capitalist domination, aiming to create a more just and egalitarian world.

Market

Market socialism is an economic system that combines elements of socialism and market mechanisms. It aims to achieve both economic efficiency and social justice by blending the advantages of a market-based economy with the equitable distribution of wealth and resources.

Market socialists argue that productive resources, such as factories and workplaces, should be socially owned or cooperatively managed. Instead of private ownership, they advocate for worker self-management, where workers have a say in decision-making and share in the profits of the enterprises they work for.

In market socialism, markets play a crucial role in determining prices and allocating resources. However, they are often subject to regulations and oversight to prevent monopolies, excessive inequality, and exploitation. The state may also intervene to provide public goods, social safety nets, and essential services.

Marxist

See Marxism.

Utopian

Utopian socialism emerged in the 19th century as an idealistic approach to social and economic reform. Its proponents sought to create egalitarian and cooperative societies, often based on communal living and shared resources. Utopian socialists believed that by eliminating the root causes of social inequality and fostering cooperation, they could achieve a more just and harmonious society.

Henri de Saint-Simon, a French philosopher and early utopian socialist, envisioned a society led by intellectuals and industrialists, with an emphasis on science and technology to improve living conditions for all. He proposed the creation of a new social order where social classes would be replaced by industrialists, scientists, and workers collaborating for the common good.

Charles Fourier, another French utopian socialist, developed the concept of phalansteries, self-sustaining and cooperative communities where work and resources were shared collectively. Fourier believed that these communities, organized around the pursuit of passions and desires, would lead to greater individual happiness and social harmony.

Étienne Cabet, a French philosopher, authored "Voyage en Icarie," describing an ideal society based on egalitarian principles and communal ownership. In his vision, private property was abolished, and economic production and distribution were collectively managed to ensure equal distribution of wealth and resources.

Robert Owen, a British social reformer and entrepreneur, believed that the environment played a crucial role in shaping individuals' behavior, and he sought to create model communities, such as New Harmony in Indiana, where cooperative living and education would lead to improved social conditions and individual well-being.

Despite their visionary ideals, utopian socialists faced criticism for their lack of concrete plans and reliance on moral persuasion rather than political action. While many of their specific communities and experiments did not last, their ideas and values left a lasting impact on socialist thought and influenced later movements that sought to address social inequality through political action and reform.

State Capitalism

State capitalism is an economic system in which the state plays a significant role in the ownership, management, and regulation of industries and businesses. Unlike traditional capitalist economies, where private ownership and market forces predominate, state capitalism involves substantial government intervention and control in key sectors of the economy.

In state capitalist systems, the government may own and operate state-owned enterprises (SOEs) in strategic industries such as energy, transportation, telecommunications, and banking. These SOEs often receive preferential treatment, subsidies, and protection from competition, giving them a dominant position in their respective markets.

State capitalism can take different forms in different countries. In some cases, it may coexist with private businesses, with the state acting as both a regulator and a market participant. In other instances, the state's role may be more extensive, with the government directly managing and controlling key industries.

Advocates of state capitalism argue that it can promote economic development, ensure long-term planning, and protect national interests in strategic sectors. They contend that state intervention can correct market failures and ensure equitable distribution of resources.

However, critics of state capitalism raise concerns about inefficiency, corruption, and lack of competition. They argue that state-controlled enterprises may be less innovative and responsive to market demands compared to private companies. Moreover, state capitalism can concentrate economic and political power in the hands of government officials, potentially leading to cronyism and favoritism.

China is often cited as an example of a country with elements of state capitalism, where the government owns and controls significant portions of the economy while also allowing for private enterprise and foreign investment. The extent of state capitalism and its implications vary widely across different countries and can be a subject of ongoing debate and analysis.

Theocracy

Theocracy is a form of government in which religious leaders or institutions hold the ultimate authority and govern in accordance with religious principles and laws. It is a unique political ideology where religious doctrine and religious leaders play a central role in shaping and governing society.

In a theocratic system, the religious principles and beliefs of a particular faith guide the laws, policies, and decision-making processes. The religious leaders, often considered to be representatives of divine authority, hold significant influence and may hold key positions of political power. Theocracy is often associated with the idea of a divine mandate, where the rulers claim to rule with the backing of a higher power.

Throughout history, various societies have adopted theocratic systems. Examples include ancient civilizations such as ancient Egypt, where the pharaohs were considered divine, and the Islamic Republic of Iran, where the country's governance is guided by Islamic principles. The Vatican City, the headquarters of the Roman Catholic Church, might also be considered a theocracy, as the Pope exercises both religious and political authority.

Advocates of theocracy argue that it provides a moral framework for governance and ensures that decisions are made in alignment with religious values. They believe that a theocratic system promotes social cohesion, morality, and stability by emphasizing religious teachings and beliefs. Theocratic societies often aim to preserve traditional values and promote religious observance, with the state playing a role in enforcing religious laws and regulations.

Critics argue that theocracy often limits freedom of thought, expression, and religious belief, as dissent or alternative interpretations may be suppressed.

Additionally, theocracy can create challenges when it comes to governance beyond religious matters. It may not adequately address the diverse needs and interests of a society, particularly when those needs conflict with religious doctrine. In contemporary times, most nations lean towards secularism, where the separation of religion and state is emphasized, and the government is considered to be neutral with respect to religious beliefs.

Theonomy

Theonomy, derived from the Greek words "theos" meaning "God" and "nomos" meaning "law," is a theological concept that revolves around the idea that society should be governed by the laws and principles found in the Bible. It is a school of thought that seeks to apply biblical teachings to all areas of life, including politics, ethics, and jurisprudence.

At its core, theonomy asserts that God's law as revealed in the Bible should serve as the ultimate standard for human conduct. Advocates of theonomy believe that God's law is not only applicable to individuals and the church but should also guide civil governance. They argue that the principles and commandments found in the Bible provide a solid foundation for a just and moral society.

One of the key figures associated with theonomy is the Reformed theologian Rousas John Rushdoony, who popularized the concept in the mid-20th century. Rushdoony argued that the Ten Commandments, along with other biblical laws and principles, should form the basis of civil legislation. He believed that society would thrive if it adhered to God's law and that this adherence would result in a restoration of moral values and societal order.

Proponents of theonomy emphasize the importance of biblical law in shaping public policy and legal systems. They argue that secular laws are often arbitrary and influenced by changing cultural norms, whereas God's law is timeless and unchanging. By adhering to theonomy, they believe that society can avoid the pitfalls of moral relativism and ensure a just and righteous order.

Transhumanism

Transhumanism is a futuristic ideology that centers around the belief in using advanced technology to enhance and transform human capabilities, both physically and mentally. It envisions a future where science and technology can be harnessed to overcome the limitations of the human condition, such as aging, disease, and even death.

At the core of transhumanism is the idea that humans should actively participate in their own evolution, using technological advancements to achieve higher levels of intelligence, longevity, and overall well-being. Proponents argue that these enhancements could lead to a post-human era, where individuals possess vastly augmented abilities and potentially even merge with artificial intelligence.

Transhumanism intersects with various fields, including artificial intelligence, genetic engineering, nanotechnology, and robotics. It raises ethical questions about the potential consequences of manipulating human biology and the social implications of a society where individuals might have unequal access to enhancements.

Critics of transhumanism express concerns about the potential for exacerbating existing inequalities, creating a divide between enhanced and non-enhanced individuals, or opening up new avenues for control and exploitation. They also raise ethical dilemmas related to the notion of "playing god" with human biology and the implications of tampering with the essence of what it means to be human.

World Federalism

World federalism is a political ideology and movement that advocates for the establishment of a global federal government to address global challenges and promote international cooperation. At its core, world federalism seeks to create a system of shared sovereignty among nations, where certain powers and responsibilities are transferred to a centralized world authority while preserving the autonomy of individual countries.

The idea of world federalism gained momentum after World War II, as a response to the devastation caused by global conflicts and the need for a more effective mechanism to prevent war and promote peace. Proponents argue that a world federal government could help prevent armed conflicts, address global issues like climate change, poverty, and human rights violations, and facilitate cooperation among nations on a wide range of issues.

The structure of a world federal government would resemble that of a federal state, with three levels of governance: local, national, and global. Local governments would manage regional affairs, national governments would oversee domestic policies, and the world federal government would handle global matters. It would have a democratic structure, where representatives from member states are elected to serve in the global legislature and make decisions through a transparent and accountable process.

Critics of world federalism raise concerns about sovereignty and the potential concentration of power in a global authority. They argue that giving up certain aspects of national sovereignty may lead to a loss of cultural identity and decision-making autonomy for individual countries. There are also practical challenges, such as ensuring representation and fair decision-making for all nations, especially those with varying sizes, resources, and political influence.

World federalists also face opposition from realist schools of international relations, which contend that global governance is unrealistic given the complexities of geopolitics and the enduring nature of national interests and power struggles.

Despite challenges, the world federalist movement continues to advocate for greater international cooperation and the establishment of global institutions to address pressing global issues. Organizations like the World Federalist Movement and the World Government Research Network work to promote the idea of a more integrated and cooperative world order.

Whiggism

Whiggism is a political ideology that emerged in England during the late 17th and 18th centuries. It represents a tradition of thought characterized by its support for constitutionalism, limited government, and the protection of individual rights and liberties.

The origins of Whiggism can be traced back to the Glorious Revolution of 1688, which saw the overthrow of King James II and the installation of William III and Mary II as joint monarchs. The Whigs, who were largely aristocrats and merchants, supported this revolution and championed parliamentary supremacy over the monarchy.

Whigs advocated for a constitutional monarchy, where the power of the monarch would be balanced by the authority of Parliament. They sought to limit the arbitrary exercise of royal power and promote the rule of law. The Glorious Revolution laid the groundwork for the Bill of Rights in 1689, which further solidified the principles of limited government, individual freedoms, and due process.

Whiggism also championed free trade, religious toleration, and the protection of property rights. It emphasized the importance of economic liberty and private enterprise as the drivers of prosperity and progress.

Throughout its history, Whiggism evolved and underwent various interpretations, and different variants emerged in different countries. In the United States, for example, Whiggism influenced the early political landscape, with figures like Henry Clay promoting policies aligned with the core Whig principles.

While Whiggism declined as a distinct political force in the 19th century, its legacy continued to influence subsequent political ideologies, particularly within liberal and conservative traditions. Its emphasis on constitutionalism, limited government, and individual rights remains an enduring feature of modern democratic thought.

Zionism

Zionism is a political and national movement that emerged in the late 19th century with the aim of establishing a Jewish homeland in the historical region of Palestine. It emerged as a response to anti-Semitism and the desire for self-determination among Jewish communities around the world.

The founder of modern political Zionism was Theodor Herzl, whose influential book "The Jewish State" (1896) outlined the need for a separate Jewish state to ensure the safety and well-being of Jews in the face of discrimination and persecution.

Zionism encompasses a range of ideologies and approaches, but the central tenet is the belief in the Jewish people's right to self-determination and their historical connection to the land of Israel. Zionists believe that a Jewish homeland is crucial for the preservation of Jewish identity, culture, and security.

The establishment of the State of Israel in 1948 marked a significant achievement for the Zionist movement. Since then, Zionism has evolved into a diverse and complex movement, encompassing religious, secular, and political expressions.

Critics of Zionism argue that it has resulted in the displacement and marginalization of Palestinian Arabs and has perpetuated an ongoing conflict. They contend that Zionism is a form of ethno-nationalism that prioritizes Jewish interests over those of other groups and undermines the rights and aspirations of Palestinians.

Supporters of Zionism argue that it is a legitimate expression of national self-determination and the fulfillment of historical and religious aspirations. They emphasize the importance of Israel as a safe haven for Jews and its contributions to science, technology, and culture.

Zionism remains a significant and contentious force in the Israeli-Palestinian conflict and continues to shape discussions surrounding the future of Israel, the rights of Palestinians, and prospects for a peaceful resolution in the region.

www.ingramcontent.com/pod-product-compliance
Lightning Source LLC
Chambersburg PA
CBHW050038260726
48658CB00005B/1666
* 9 7 9 8 8 5 1 8 1 6 1 1 6 *